Better Choices, Better Life

How to Eliminate Your Self-Defeating Behaviors and Live a Happier Life

by Carol Bettino, M.A.

Better Choices, Better Life
Published   by:

BLUE BIRD PUBLISHING
2266 S. Dobson, Suite #275
Mesa AZ 85202
(602) 831-6063
FAX (602) 831-1829
Email: bluebird@bluebird1.com
Web site: http://www.bluebird1.com

The names and identities of the persons used in this book
have been changed to protect their confidentiality.

ISBN 0-933025-76-9
$14.95

CONTENTS

DEDICATION:

To My Husband, Jim.
You have always supported me in everything
I have ever done. You were, and always will be
"the wind beneath my wings."
I love you ......

To My Children, Jay and Gina
You are very loving and sensitive.
In a world with such turbulence,
I couldn't ask for better children.
I am very proud of both of you.
I love you with all my heart.

ABOUT THE AUTHOR

Carol Bettino, M.A., C.P.C. has been helping people eliminate self-defeating behaviors from their lives for many years. As a therapist and board certified professional counselor, she has been involved with this field since 1984. Carol has designed and conducted numerous workshops such as, "Getting Unstuck: Eliminating Self-Defeating Behavior," "Helping Clients with Fear, Anxiety and Panic Disorders," "How to Raise Children Without Shame," "Eliminating Self-Defeating Behavior: Independence from Co-Dependency," and many more. She teaches college level courses in psychology, parenting, self-esteem, and elminating self-defeating behaviors. Her professional work experience includes the prestigious Charter Hospital as well as Valley Youth Organization, and Faith House (a shelter for women), all located in Phoenix. She is currently in private practice with the Arizona Community Psychiatric Group in Phoenix.

SPECIAL THANKS AND ACKNOWLEDGMENTS

A special thanks to my wonderful and loving parents, who taught me to believe that I could do anything I set my mind to. Their guidance and support has never led me astray. Their love, values, and faith will live in my heart forever. Until we meet again in God's kingdom, I love and miss you both.

To My Husband, Jim, and children Jay and Gina.
You are my life, my inspiration and my dreams. I thank you for your love, support, humor, and uncanny way of always making me feel special.

To My Best Friend, Paula Williams.
Even though we are at opposite ends of the map, you are always there for me. Your friendship has seen me through many ups and downs. My life has been blessed because of our friendship.

To my sisters, Jeannie, Theresa and Mary Kay.
Thank you for reading my manuscript. A special thanks for believing in me, encouraging and supporting me to continue. Thanks for being good friends and wonderful sisters.

To Sean McDevitt, Ph.D.
My sincerest appreciation for reading and re-reading my manuscript. You were always so gracious when I cornered you in the halls and gave you a new chapter. I am very grateful for your editorial comments, changes and direction. Your support and guidance was instrumental in getting this book published.

To Mabel Hurley.
I never even met you, yet you unselfishly took the time to voluntarily edit my manuscript so I can send it to the publishers in a more polished, professional manner. Thank you.

To Vivian Jean Lasher.
Thank you for printing every revised copy. My printer would surely have died for the amount of times I have revised this book. I sincerely appreciate your help.

To Betty Della-Corte Ryan and Faith House.
I thank you for the opportunity to turn a volunteer job into an internship of learning. I will forever be grateful.

To Dennis & Donna Betz.
Thank you for your computer knowledge and help in transferring my archaic disk onto a modern disk that would read my manuscript.

To all the people that have touched and enriched my life.
My family, my grandmother, my brothers, sisters, nieces, nephews, godmother, friends, clients and students. To my mentors, Joann Rice and Betty Carnes who have inspired me. Thank you all from deep within my heart.

To My God, My Savior, Jesus Christ, and My Guardian Angels. Without You, nothing would be possible. Thank You. I praise You for your undying love, and for always carrying me when I needed You, especially during the most painful times of my life.

PREFACE

I began this book in 1991. I was creating lectures for my college class, *Eliminating Self-Defeating Behaviors*. I sent it out for publication and was turned down by about six publishers. I revised it and sent it out again, only to have it rejected some more. I had so much positive feedback from my students about my lectures, I knew I had to find a better way to make my notes come alive in book form. So in 1994 I picked it up again. I made more changes, additions and deletions. Again I sent it out and again it was rejected. My ego doesn't bruise that easily. I read that Richard Hooker, writer of the war novel *M*A*S*H* was rejected by 21 publishers before it was published. I knew I was no Richard Hooker, but I knew I had something that people would benefit by. So, in 1996, with the feedback from my friend and colleague, Sean McDevitt, I began to teach the lecture aloud to my archaic computer, attempting to put into book form what was in my head and heart. Sean helped me stay focused on outlines and formats. My sister Jeannie's friend offered her mother's services who happened to be a retired editor. God bless Mabel, she polished it up so I could send it off again. This time felt different. My direction was different and my manuscript more organized (thanks to Sean). Even my words were clearer, like a real writer (thanks to Mabel).

This book is not a panacea for self-defeating behaviors. It is however, a book about personal introspective understanding and personal growth. There are many helpful hints, Do's and Don't's, and direction to help eliminate self-defeating behaviors. I believe it is a positive approach to negative issues.

My intention is to let you know that regardless of your past experiences, you control your destiny. You do not have to recreate your history or stay in bad situations because of underlying fears. You are responsible for the way you think, feel and act. Do not get trapped in your problems or your past. Look for solutions. If you need help, seek it. Don't spend wasteless time complaining about it. Reading this book is just a step. A step for personal change and personal growth. Your future is what you make it. This book will give you an opportunity to learn how to eliminate your self-defeating behaviors.

A thought by Whitney Young, Jr.

> **"It is better to be prepared for an opportunity and not have one than to have an opportunity and not be prepared."**

Open your mind, move forward and take charge of your thoughts, feelings and behaviors. Eliminate your self-defeating behaviors now.

Journey of Recovery
by Carol Bettino

Recovery is far from perfect—
you will find no easy roads.
It sometimes feels overwhelming
when the pain of the past unfolds.

Don't make excuses or blame everyone else.
That will keep you from finding your true self.
Give yourself permission, to feel which you must
to learn to love yourself, you must begin with trust.

Trust your instincts and your feelings too.
Never allow anyone to ever invalidate you.
The journey's road has twists and turns
for there are many loving lessons to learn.

Don't give up when the pain overwhelms you.
Reach out to someone who will teach you to love you.
Begin your journey by asking God to be your guide.
He'll be there to carry you, until the pain subsides.

INTRODUCTION

Self-defeating behavior is any behavior that interferes with the person's healthy functioning and development. To understand self-defeating behaviors, you must understand why you behave or react the way you do. Once you understand it, your goal is to eliminate those unwanted behaviors. If you don't understand why you do what you do, or why you react the way you do, you risk recreating the same problems and engaging in self-defeating behaviors. Learning from your past experience means not having to repeat it.

In the poem "Attitude," Charles Swindoll wrote, "Life is 10% what happens to me and 90% how I react to it". A person's **reactions** to the things that actually happen in life determine whether that person will be happy and productive. This book is about learning to deal with everyday problems and experience feelings without engaging in self-defeating thinking or behavior. You will learn how to handle problems and simple everyday mistakes differently. You will learn how to recognize the warning signs of self-defeating behaviors in their early stages and how to eliminate those behaviors by changing your reactions. You will learn to deal with feelings instead of stuffing or ignoring them. You will learn more about yourself and how your past experiences have affected your life. You will like and respect yourself more. The way you think and feel determines your behavior.

Chapter 1 will help you see how past experiences have affected your life. You will see how carrying baggage can prevent you from going where you want to go, doing what you want to do, and being what you want to be. Your history is not your destiny.

10

Chapter 2 defines self-defeating behaviors. It will give common examples of self-defeating behaviors and helpful techniques to eliminate them.

Chapter 3 teaches you to identify, express and experience feelings. You will begin to journal your own feelings and memories and see how they have impacted you. You will learn the difference between healthy feelings and overwhelming feelings. You will learn to control your feelings instead of your feelings controlling you.

Chapter 4 differentiates between healthy guilt and shame and debilitating or crippling guilt and shame. It helps you see the underlying reasons for some of your self-defeating behaviors. It will help you take control and responsibility for your thoughts and behaviors.

Chapter 5 is about boundaries. You will learn how to set limits and stand up for yourself. If you have a difficult time saying "no" now, you won't when you finish this chapter.

Chapter 6 is about self-esteem. Whether you never had it or it was damaged, you will rebuild it better than before. You'll learn about yourself, your needs, and what's important to you.

Chapter 7 is about communicating in assertive ways. You will learn about your basic rights and how to assert yourself to gain the respect you deserve. You will also be able to differentiate between aggressive and assertive communication.

Chapter 8 is about attitude and how that plays a part in your life. You will utilize a a simple 1-2-3 approach to help you understand and change your problems, reactions, attitude and feelings.

Chapter 9 is about relationships. You will see the difference between healthy and unhealthy relationships. You will know the Ten Commandments of a loving relationship.

Chapter 10 is about finding a balance. You will learn to avoid extremes. You will take what you need from what you learn and discard what doesn't fit. You won't have all the answers, but <u>you'll recognize</u> them when you see them.

While you are reading this book, any time something such as an emotion, memory or self-defeating thought or behavior is triggered within you or you can relate to a passage, stop and write about it. Question yourself on how you can handle it differently. Question what has to change, and how are you going to change it. This type of journaling is a method you will use throughout this book.

Journaling helps you to understand your feelings and reactions. It is nothing more than transferring what is in your head onto paper, keeping a diary. On a daily basis, write down your feelings, thoughts, reactions and behaviors. Write about how you want to make change and what changes you intend to make. At the end of the week, reread your journal. Learn from it and make change happen. Don't get stuck in the problems. Understand them, and look for solutions.

When you journal, you get things off your chest and eliminate nagging thoughts from your mind. A journal validates your feelings by exposing what you think and how you feel. It makes the unconscious, conscious, and you can face your feelings instead of feeling overwhelmed. That's why talking to someone about your problem makes you feel like a burden has been lifted and you feel better. It's also why prayer works. By rereading, you validate your reality. The facts are out, the emotions are under control. You see things from a clearer perspective. This allows you to be more objective and make conscious choices when dealing with solutions to a problem, instead of overreacting to a situation or a problem.

In your journal, write a list of some self-defeating behaviors you think you may have or be using.

Write down what you want to change in your thinking and yourself.

_____
_____
_____

 Why do you react in a self-defeating way? (What are the thoughts, feelings or beliefs that trigger your reaction?)

_____
_____
_____

What can you do differently? (Can you change the way you think or feel, your attitude, reactions, behaviors?)_____
_____
_____
_____

   Keep in mind, the choices you make, good or bad, will have consequences. Engaging in self-defeating behaviors is not an accident. Learn to think things out before you act on something. Do not allow your feelings to control you. Control your feelings. You will think clearer and make better decisions when you are in control of emotions.

   WARNING: If you feel suicidal or are in a dangerous situation, seek professional help immediately. There are local agencies and hotlines in every state. Call information for a community service hotline or agency. A book is not enough! It is only a step.

Chapter One

Letting Go Of Baggage

- *Chapter One* -

Letting Go Of Baggage

Baggage, what is it? It's the faulty messages, beliefs, unresolved issues and feelings, hurt and pain from past experiences. Lucky
people go through life with one piece of baggage. Everyone has baggage. Some baggage is heavier than others or there are more pieces.
Some of us may carry the hidden baggage of traumatic or painful
memories. Others may take on another person's baggage and take
responsibility for it, carrying everybody else's baggage. You may
carry baggages of "what ifs," "shoulda's," "coulda's" and "oughta's."
There is baggage for every feeling and every unresolved issue. The
goal is to get rid of excessive baggage and take responsibility for
yourself and your life. It's like cleaning out a closet. You go through
the closet getting rid of what doesn't fit and what you don't want
anymore. Some things just need to be thrown away. If not disposed
of, it prevents you from going where you want to go and doing what
you want to do in life. Doris's experience is an example.

Doris is at the airport and has the opportunity to go anywhere
she wants to go. The only restriction is that she can only take "one
bag per person." Because she has too much baggage, she can't go on
the plane. Ignoring how she really feels, and what a healthy reaction
would be she pretends she'd rather take a bus instead. She is beginning to learn how to settle for less than she wants and convince her-

self that it doesn't matter. She walks away from the plane saying, "I'd rather take the bus anyway." She sees the sign above the bus "one bag per person." She is disappointed and angry. Yelling and screaming at the bus driver, she storms away and almost knocks an old man over. She yells at the man for getting in her way. She sees the train. Attempting to board the train, she sees the same sign. At this point she feels defeated and alone. She feels sorry for herself. She wants to run away. She looks around at the other people in the station. They all appear to be going where they want to go. Why can't she? She feels overwhelmed.

She feels desperate to get rid of this painful feeling. She sees a taxi and thinks "I'll do anything and pay any price to get out of here." (The symbolism of the taxi can be, alcohol, drugs, food, overspending. It can be someone or something.) She approaches the taxi driver. He says, "I can drive you around the airport as many times as you like but I can't take you where you want to go unless you get rid of the extra baggage."

Doris has a choice to get rid of the extra baggage so she can get on with her life, but because she can't or doesn't want to face the decision she's trapped into desperate measures and even those don't work.

Everybody has baggage. You have to decide which ones are preventing you from going where you want to go and being who you want to be. You have to take ownership of your baggage and the responsibility for it. You cannot blame others if you choose to carry their baggage. You can't blame past experiences for your self-defeating behaviors. You choose what beliefs to carry and you choose what action to take based on those beliefs. Your past experiences has affected and impacted your life. However, to what extent will you allow it to continue to direct your life? You have choices. Your history does not have to be your destiny. Now is a good time to look through your baggage. As you go through it, decide what to let go of. Can you think of some issues that are baggage for you?

This would be a good time to journal what thoughts or feelings come up.

When you make a mistake or do something you consider stupid, it's amazing what thoughts go through your head. You react to things based on how you feel. If you feel exposed when you make a mistake, it triggers uncomfortable feelings. If someone saw you do it, you feel embarrassed. You may unconsciously obsess about what you did and what someone thinks about you because of it. This may even trigger other uncomfortable feelings. Your thinking may become distorted. You feel as if your mistake is going to be televised on national TV or in the newspaper. For example, feelings of fear can be overwhelming at times. You may fear being vulnerable, feeling inferior or feeling stupid, or you may fear what others think. Such fears can immobilize you. The experience of Cindy, a student of mine, illustrates this.

Cindy shared that her fear of speaking in front of the class for her three minute presentation was so overwhelming that she experienced extreme anxiety and contemplated dropping the class. She was afraid she would say something stupid. I reminded her what I kept telling the class, "CNN news will not show up and televise your presentation." She smiled, yet her fear was very real. I asked her to journal about her fears and things in her life that she was afraid of. I asked her to journal about embarrassing times and how she handled them, and how others reacted to her mistakes. She handed me her journal two weeks later. As a child she had been disciplined severely anytime she did something wrong or made a mistake.

Making a mistake, especially in front of others, had extremely overwhelming consequences for her. Her current fears were not just about appearing stupid, they were about feeling like a little kid again and being overwhelmingly afraid of embarrassment. I reminded her that in making her presentation, the worst that could happen would be that she say something stupid and someone would laugh. CNN wouldn't storm through the door. The person's laughing wouldn't mean she was stupid. I also reminded her that she was an adult, not a child. That was then, and this is now. I helped her see that she had choices and she was not powerless. I validated her fear as a child. I explained that as a child she didn't have choices, and the consequences of her mistakes were severe. They were also unjustified. I then helped her see that her past did not have to control her life anymore.

In her journal, she wrote that she had always felt inferior, less than and not as good as others. She was afraid to pursue any promotions at work. She was a people pleaser, even at the expense of doing things she didn't want just so people would like her. She would let anyone take advantage of her because she didn't want anyone to be angry with her. She felt stupid and at fault whenever anything went wrong. Writing these things in her journal opened her eyes. She realized she was basing her adult life on the faulty beliefs and irrational feelings (unnecessary baggage) of a child.

Cindy made her presentation ten weeks later (she was the last one). Before she stood up in front of the class, she did a quick imagery of seeing herself as an adult and as a child. The adult went to the child and told her to go play and have fun while the adult stood up before the class. Her quick imagery worked. Her opening statement was "I'm nervous and I'm afraid, but Carol promised me CNN won't come through the door." The class laughed. Cindy smiled and continued her presentation. She was still afraid, but she didn't let her fear stand in the way. She faced her fear that day. She moved on instead of letting her past fears determine the direction of her life. Everybody is afraid of making mistakes, especially in front of other people. For Cindy, it was an intense fear which she had carried from childhood. You don't have to be immobilized by fear. You can face your fear and do it anyway. As the NIKE slogan suggests "Just do it."

This is a good time to do some journaling. Write down your past and current fears, listing embarrassing times, how you dealt with them and how others reacted to them. After a few days, go back and read your journal entry. Then list new thoughts, reactions and attitude about those fears and what techniques you will use to handle them now.

Fears/Embarrassment	How I Reacted	How Others Reacted
_____	_____	_____
_____	_____	_____
_____	_____	_____

Here is a simple ABC quiz to follow when you make a minor mistake. "Okay, you missed the exit because you weren't paying attention and now you're 5 minutes late," or "you forgot to pick up the clothes from the dry cleaners and now they are closed. What should you do?"

A) Hire a hitman or a firing squad.

B) Punish yourself for 30 days constantly reminding yourself how stupid you are. Criticize yourself, put yourself down every chance you get. Have nightmares about it. If you start enjoying yourself, remind yourself of how stupid you are or ...

C) Deal with it and its consequences. Take responsibility and apologize if appropriate. Make amends if you have to, but forget it. Let it go and move on with your life. You have a choice. You can be miserable, angry or upset all day or let it go.

Like Dorothy in the *Wizard of Oz*, you come to a point in the road where there is more than one choice to make. Each choice, good or bad, impacts your life and has consequences. There are no guarantees that the choice you make will be the right one. Sometimes, you may be so afraid of making the wrong choice that you don't make any. This is self-defeating.

Self-defeating behavior is never a healthy response to failure, a mistake or a difficulty in handling feelings. Mistakes are opportunities to learn. The truth is, no one is perfect. The legendary Hall of Famer, Babe Ruth, who held a record for hitting 714 homeruns, also struck out 1,330 times. The choice is, which record do you emphasize?

When things don't work out the way you want, your attitude will determine how you respond. If you let fear of rejection or fear of failure stand in your way, you may give up too soon. Even the talented Walt Disney went bankrupt several times before he built Disneyland. Seven publishers rejected my book before it was published. If you let negative thoughts permeate your thinking, your focus will be on what you can't do, instead of what you can do. Henry Ford said, **"Whether you think you can or whether you think you can't, either way, you're right."** Again, the choice is yours.

Many of you go through life carrying a bag of **"what ifs."** What if Dorothy had gone in another direction and never met the scarecrow, the tinman and the lion? Would she have ever found the "Land of Oz?" No one knows. Carrying a bag of **"what ifs"** can keep you trapped and very unhappy. There is no guarantee that if it were different, it would have been better.

My Baggage   Why I Should Let It Go
_____   _____
_____   _____

To insure you to move on with your life and let go of your mistakes, failures, and old baggage, I'd like to quote Aldous Huxley:

**"Experience is not what happens to a man.
It is what a man does with what happens to him."**

Chapter Two

Understanding Self-Defeating Behavior

- *Chapter Two* -

Understanding Self-Defeating Behavior

Self-defeating behavior is any behavior that interferes with a person's healthy functioning and development. To change self-defeating behaviors, you first need to understand what is causing them. Why are you acting in a self-defeating way? This does not always mean that you need therapy or have to analyze everything you say and do. If you overreact more often than not, it would be helpful to explore why. If you cannot discriminate between what is important and what is trivial, you need to determine the reason. You may be too stressed, too emotional or carrying too much baggage.

A problem-solving approach helps better understand self-defeating behaviors. Break down the process into smaller and easier parts. Here are some simple steps to eliminate self-defeating behaviors.

First, recognize you have a problem and decide what to do about it. Identify your self-defeating behavior(s). Examples might be having a bad temper or mentally or verbally abusing others when you are frustrated.

Second, own the behavior. <u>Admit</u> the behavior is yours. Take the behavior seriously. You have a problem if you can't control your emotions. If you intimidate, yell or get physical when you are angry, it's your problem. "They" didn't make you do it. Don't blame others or make excuses for your behavior.

Third, <u>take responsibility </u>for the behavior. Apologize when appropriate. Make amends if needed. Make a conscious choice to do something about the behavior. For example, join a support group or a 12 Step meeting, take a class, make a plan, or seek help.

Fourth, try to understand your feelings. Talk to someone about the problem, journal about it. <u>Question</u> yourself, look at your family history. You may be recreating what you have learned as a child. That's not an excuse, it's an observation. Support groups can be helpful.

Fifth, stop the behavior immediately. Learn from it, don't repeat the behavior. <u>Focus</u> on changing or eliminating the behavior. If you have tried on your own to change the behavior and it hasn't worked, use the steps in this book.

If you worked on your own car and you couldn't fix it, wouldn't you go to a mechanic? That doesn't mean you are stupid. Some jobs are harder than others. A professional outside perspective can help you see things differently. There is no shame in getting help. If you have shame about it, you need to open your baggage and get rid of the faulty belief that is preventing you from seeking help.

Dealing with feelings when you are already under a lot of pressure can be emotionally painful. If you don't deal with stress well, or if you deny your feelings, you are at high risk to engage in self-defeating behaviors. This is not an excuse, it is an observation.

As mentioned earlier, for a behavior to be self-defeating, it must interfere with the person's healthy functioning and development. Let's use drinking as an example. Your drinking is causing marital problems. You may be late for work or miss work because of your drinking. Maybe you're not spending time with your children because you are with friends drinking. You may be emotionally absent to your family. Your failure to deal with these situations can cause emotional, psychological and physiological problems. Although you may think your self-defeating behavior affects only you, that is rarely true. It almost always causes problems and tension within the family and the work environment. When others bring your behavior to your attention, you should think it through.

Another example is the workaholic. Mike was working 12 to 14 hours a day 6 to 7 days a week. His wife was overwhelmed with taking care of the household chores and their two children. The couple began to fight every time they were together. He began to work more to avoid fighting. The children were sleeping when he came home and when he left. He missed every family function. One night Mike thought he was having a heart attack. He was rushed to the hospital. It was a panic attack. His excessive work hours nearly destroyed him and his family. He was unable to see the effects until it was almost too late.

Here are a few other examples of the many common self-defeating behaviors and personality characteristics (This is not an exhaustive list.)

✎ **CONTROLLING** - Attempt to control everyone and everything. When there is loss of control, uses coercion, guilt tactics, physical force, manipulation, threats or domination to gain control.

✎ **DEPENDENCY** - Fear of being alone. Latches onto anyone or anything for happiness. Feels trapped, helpless, or unhappy in their relationships or career but feels helpless or afraid to get out. Jumps from one problem to another or one relationship to another. Would rather be in a bad relationship than no relationship at all.

26

✎ **WORRYING** - Feel responsible for taking care of everyone and everything for fear that something will go wrong. Worries about everyone and everything and always questions what will happen next and "what if." Obsesses about everything and always looks for the negative and the worst that could happen.

✎ **LACK OF TRUST** - Does not trust self, feelings, instincts, decisions, thoughts or beliefs. Has no trust or faith in anyone or anything. Feels life is externally controlled by other people and things that happen. Is fearful of being vulnerable and so stays very guarded.

✎ **REPRESSING FEELINGS** - Stuffs or freezes feelings. Fears appearing vulnerable, weak, out of control, or getting hurt. These people feel they have no right to feel the way they do, so they cover up their feeling by wearing an "I'm OK" pretend mask or "I don't care" mask. They share very little of themselves.

✎ **LOSS OF TEMPER** - Becomes abusive or violent when control of self or situation is lost. When frustrated, has hostile physical or verbal outbursts that affect and frighten those around them. These people have carried guilt and anger for so long, they blame everyone and everything for their outbursts. anything can trigger their anger.

✎ **EXCESSIVE CARETAKING** - Takes responsibility for other people, their feelings and their problems even though the other people can take care of themselves. These people overextend themselves, do for others when they don't want to, or at the risk of hurting themselves. They resent doing things, feel and act like martyrs or victims.

✎ **PERFECTIONISM** - Expects and demands perfection in self and everyone else. Becomes very critical of self and others. Nothing ever seems good enough. These people continue to seek approval from others or demand that others seek their approval. They never get approval, nor do they give it.

✎ **COMPULSIVE BEHAVIORS -** Alcohol or drug abuse, abusing prescription drugs, gambling, overeating, anorexia, bulimia, excessive dieting or exercising, overspending and shopping, obsessive cleaning, physically abusing others, and any obsessive thinking that leads to compulsive behaviors.

✎ (Place your self-defeating behaviors here and give examples:

_____
_____
_____

What is the difference between a self-defeating behavior and an addiction? According to Dr. Lisa Sparks, an Arizona physician specializing in addiction medicine, "An addiction is a disease process characterized by the continued use of a specific psycho-active substance, despite physical, psychological or social harm." A self-defeating behavior is any behavior that is causing physical and/or psychological harm as well as interfering with the person's functioning and development. The problem is, many people don't see their own behavior as self defeating. A rule of thumb is, if everyone sees it but you, look harder.

Self-defeating behaviors can be changed or eliminated through education and awareness. (i.e) Taking classes, attending seminars, support groups, 12 Step meetings, hypnosis, biofeedback, reading, counseling or therapy. If your behavior causes problems in your life, affects your family's life, or is a danger to yourself or others, seek professional help immediately. Using the example of the car, imagine your car constantly breaking down. What would happen if you ignored it? The problem wouldn't go away; it would get worse. The bigger the problem, the harder it is to fix.

Here are some simple helpful hints to eliminate self-defeating behaviors.

✓ Place a rubber band around your wrist. Whenever you think about or engage in negative or faulty thinking or behavior, snap the rubber band. Say to yourself as you snap the rubber band, "This hurts me or my family, I don't want to do it. I need to stop, it hurts too much." Eventually, you get the hint.

✓ Write down your thoughts, feelings and behaviors. This can help you detect a pattern and a link between thinking and behavior. A few hours or a few days later, look at what you wrote. It will give you insight and a better perspective.

✓ Solicit people for help. Tell them you are trying to stop a behavior. Ask them to bring negative behavior to your attention in a positive way. (e.g., Carol, didn't you want me to remind you if you were being controlling? Just say thank you.) At this point, talk yourself through it and get out of the negative behavior.

✓ List your negative thoughts, beliefs and behaviors. At the end of the day, look at that list. If you engaged in any of those behaviors, make a plan on how to change them. List ways how you will avoid those behaviors the next time. Follow your plan and revise it as needed.

✓ Have a two-way conversation with yourself. Don't worry. This doesn't mean you have a split personality. You can be your own worst enemy at times. You need to learn to be your own best friend. During your two-way conversation, challenge your faulty beliefs. Give yourself suggestions. Be compassionate and understanding to yourself. Talk to yourself as you would to someone you love.

✓ Attend support groups. There are many support groups that are free in the community. Be with others who experience similar problems. Seek professional help if you need it. Attend a class and learn more about yourself and self-defeating behaviors. Read self-help books.

✓ Write letters to people you are angry with or have been hurt by or are annoyed with. **Don't** mail them. Do it for yourself. Say what is on your mind. Get it off your chest. Go ahead, let them have it. Even if it is trivial, it feels good to get it out. When you're done, throw the letter away, burn it, or rip it into tiny pieces. Just get rid of it. The goal is to let it go, not hold on to it.

✓ While you are taking a shower, tell everybody off that annoyed you that day or the day before. If someone is in the house with you say it under your breath. Just keep talking until you have nothing more to say about it. Once it's out, you feel less burdened. It is also easier to put things in perspective, not personalize everything and not feel as overwhelmed by trivial things.

✓ Use exercise or physical activity to get rid of pent up energy. Sometimes you only need to do it for a few minutes. After exercising, begin using relaxation techniques (e.g., breathing; imaging or visualizing safe, relaxing, beautiful places; yoga; meditation; and, of course, prayer).

✓ Eat and drink healthy. Modify your sugar and caffeine intake. Avoid alcohol and other mood altering drugs. Too much of anything can eventually cause problems.

✓ Challenge your negative thoughts. Underneath many self-defeating behaviors lie shame which will be covered later. If you have grown up in an abusive home, or had a bad experience while growing up, you may be carrying old dysfunctional, negative tapes. These negative messages may attack your self-worth, identity and self-esteem. You must challenge these messages every time they come up. You can choose what you take from your past and what you leave behind. Most of these messages you give to yourself. (e.g.,) "I'm so stupid," "I can't do anything right." Challenge it! Change the message.

✓ Take control over how you think, how you feel and how you react. When you are in charge, these thoughts and negative messages can no longer control you. You control them. Learn to "dismiss" them.

Say the word "dismissed" out loud or to yourself, as many times as you need to. When a judge says "dismissed," it's over. Anyone else can say what they want, but they won't be heard because the judge is in charge. Take charge of your life, "dismiss" unwanted thoughts and messages. Don't expect that one word uttered just a few times will change years of thinking. Keep saying it, keep practicing, eventually it will work.

Abuse is any form of mistreatment. Abuse can occur in relationships with significant others, work relationships (i.e., boss/employee or co-worker/co-worker, parent/child relationships, parent/adult child relationships) and in any adult sibling or friendship relationships. When abuse occurs, at any level, it damages your self esteem and self worth.

Negative messages have negative effects. No one goes throughout life without negative messages coming from somewhere or someone. Take a moment now to list the negative messages you have received throughout your life, including the most recent, whether they be from parents, friends, relatives, teachers, counselors, coaches, siblings, or even day-to-day relationships. These messages and beliefs have been in your baggage whether for a day or years.

Before I graduated from eighth grade I took tests to see what parochial high school I would attend. I wanted to attend a new high school that had just been built. When my tests came back, I didn't make the high school. I made a 3 year commercial high school for girls. (I'm giving away my age, they don't have those schools anymore.) I went to my counselor at school. I cried. I was disappointed and ashamed because so many of my friends made the high school I wanted to go to. The counselor said "Carol, some people aren't college material. Your grades are just not good enough, you're not college material. A commercial high school will be good for you." Whether she meant well or not, those words stayed with me for many years.

I was 25 years old when I registered for college. That was 11 years later, that voice nearly stopped me. I was scared when I asked for an application to attend college. I sat down, nervous, trying to stop the voice in my head that said "You're not college material." After I wrote my name on the top of the application, the next line had the word "Nee." I froze, I looked at the door and thought, "I'm not college material. I should just leave." Another voice said to ask what Nee meant. I did, the lady smiled and said, "It means any former names, like your maiden name." I faced my fear that day. I had other questions. I challenged that voice from my baggage and I asked the questions. I received answers and I finished filling out my application. Ten years later, I graduated with a Masters Degree in Education in Counseling. This is an example that no voice within or outside will prevent you from going where you want, unless you let it.

Now decide which messages you choose to keep and which ones you choose to get rid of. Also, look to see how some of them have already affected your life in a negative way. Then remind yourself that you are not helpless. You have control over your life. If you have learned bad habits as a way of coping, you can also unlearn them. You can change your attitude, thinking, reactions and your behavior.

Eliminating self-defeating behavior is taking responsibility for your life. It is moving from a victim or martyr role of self pity, in which you feel it's "anybody and everybody's fault" for my problems, to a responsible role of "If I don't like it, then I must do something to change it." I saw a poster that simply said, **"Misery is optional."** It's true, we do have choices and our attitude plays a big part in the choices we make.

What negative messages have you carried?

_____

_____

_____

What messages are you going to get rid of and what are you going to do about changing them?

_____

_____

_____

What self-defeating behaviors do you need to change?

_____

_____

_____

Write an example of how you let a negative message affect your behavior.

_____

_____

_____

What thoughts and messages were going through your head?

_____

_____

_____

What were you feeling?

_____

_____

_____

How did you react?

_____

_____

_____

How did you deal with your reaction?

_____

_____

_____

What would you like to change?

_____
_____
_____

Don't stay trapped in self-defeating or self-destructive thinking or behaviors because of what someone in the past said or did. While it is true that your past experiences plays a part and contributes to the way you think, feel and act, your past does not have to determine the way you think, feel or act in your present. You are <u>not</u> powerless over the decisions and choices you make in your life.

Practice telling yourself daily, **"I AM IN CHARGE OF <u>MY</u> LIFE AND <u>MY</u> DESTINY."**

Imagine how the world would have been different if the following people carried and lived by the beliefs of others.

✳ **Beethoven's music teacher called him "hopeless as a composer."**

✳ **Albert Einstein's teacher called him "mentally slow and unsociable."**

✳ **Professional hockey player Wayne Gretzky was told he was too small and didn't weigh enough to be a hockey player.**

✳ **Walt Disney was told "he lacked ideas." That is why he was fired by a newspaper editor.**

No one but yourself can keep you trapped by negative messages.   Remember, just because someone says it, doesn't mean it's true.

I would like to end the chapter with the following poem:

Autobiography in 5 Short Chapters by Portia Nelson

l

I walk down the street, there is a deep hole in the sidewalk.
I fall in I am lost, I am helpless, It isn't my fault,
It takes forever to find a way out.

ll

I walk down the same street, there is a deep hole in the sidewalk
I pretend I don't see it, I fall again, I can't believe I am in the same
place, but it isn't my fault. It still takes a long time to get out.

lll

I walk down the same street there is a deep hole in the sidewalk. I see
it there, I still fall in, it's a habit, my eyes are open, I know where I
am, It is my fault, I get out immediately.

IV

I walk down the same street there is a deep hole in the sidewalk, I
walk around it.

V

I walk down another street.

Chapter Three

How to Understand and Deal with Overwhelming Feelings

- *Chapter Three* -

How to Understand and Deal with Overwhelming Feelings

This chapter is about overwhelming feelings. As you read this chapter, journal any feelings, thoughts or memories that come up for you. Especially list feelings you have ignored or covered up.

Feelings are a natural part of human experience. Feelings are not judged right or wrong or good or bad. However, what you do with your feelings and how you express them can be. It is a natural reaction to cry and be sad when someone dies. It is not a healthy reaction to isolate, stay in bed, and avoid day to day functioning because of your sadness. It's okay to get angry, but it is unacceptable to hurt someone else or destroy something because you are angry.

List some times when you were overwhelmed by feelings.
1._____
2._____
3._____

How did you handle your feelings?

1._____

2._____

3._____

How could you have handled it better?

1._____

2._____

3._____

To understand how feelings react when contained, picture a pot on the stove with boiling water. If you cover it, water overflows and makes a mess. You must lower the heat. Everyone has overwhelming feelings at times. Covering up or ignoring feelings does not make them stop. The feelings brew and eventually someone or something triggers them, you become overwhelmed, and then overreact.

Now imagine an emotional volcano with bubbling lava within you. When you are emotionally healthy, your threshold is low. Therefore, when something upsets you, you deal with it without feeling overwhelmed. When you deny your feelings, they bubble inside, and the threshold rises. If the threshold is too high, any trigger can make it erupt. It's the proverbial straw that breaks the camel's back.

normal threshold

unhealthy threshold

If you don't learn to deal with feelings in healthy ways, you become overwhelmed. Your feelings control you instead of you controlling your feelings. There are many unfortunate stories about people who went on killing sprees because they were overwhelmed and lost control. It is evident that the loss of control was not just about being angry at a person or a situation. The anger triggered their volcano and they lost control. At that point there is no logical or rational thinking.

In the movie *Falling Down*, with Michael Douglas, everything was going wrong. He was overwhelmed. He was no longer able to handle stress. He became a danger to himself and others. He was irrational and out of control. When the convenience store clerk wouldn't make change, he became violent, started shooting and destroying the store. By itself, not having enough change to make a phone call is not enough to make a volcano erupt. But by not dealing with his emotions, he became so overwhelmed that anything, no matter how minor, could trigger an eruption.

If you don't face your feelings, they will become part of your baggage. If you deny them, they continue to bubble waiting for an eruption. It's only a matter of time when the baggage becomes too heavy or a minor trigger makes the volcano erupt.

The chart below came from numerous workshops I attended, most cited the originator as Pia Melody, author of *Facing Codependency*. They gave examples of carried feelings and how feelings get trapped within the body.

Feeling	Feeling Reality	Carried/Overwhelmed Feeling
Anger	Control/Energy	Rage/Abuse/Violence
Fear	Protection	Panic/Anxiety/Paranoia
Sadness	Growth	Depression/Despair
Guilt	Fallibility/Humanness	*Crippling sense of shame

* A feeling of worthlessness, feeling useless, defective, damaged, inadequate, inferior, dumb, bad, just not good enough.

In the list above, you see everyday emotions that people experience. Anger/frustration, sadness/hurt, fear/worry and guilt/shame. Feelings have energy. They can bubble for a long time before erupting. The reality of anger is control. When you don't control your anger, you lose control. The pent-up energy of anger is like bubbling lava. It only takes one little trigger, no matter how insignificant, to erupt an overwhelming reaction or even an abusive blind rage.

ANGER

When my mother died, my 14 year old daughter was devastated. She was very close to my mother. One night, I approached her concerning her feelings about losing her grandmother. At first, she didn't want to talk about it. She broke down and cried. We both cried and held each other. Then she told me she was angry at God. She had prayed on her rosary beads and asked God to make her grandmother better. She was angry because He hadn't. I validated her feelings. I let her know that it was okay to get angry at God because He would never turn His back on her. He also would understand how she felt. I told her that her grandmother prayed on her rosary beads, too, and maybe God had answered her prayers instead. We both cried again. By helping her see her feelings were okay, she was able to let go of the anger and begin to deal with her grief and pain about losing her grandmother. She later told me that she and God were friends again.

I've known many people who have lost their faith during painful times of their lives, only because they don't know that what they are feeling is normal. By talking about your feelings you understand more. You can then let go of the anger, pain or sadness and move on with your life. The goal is not to get stuck in your feelings. You learn to control your feelings, instead of your feelings controlling you.

This may be a good time for you to journal feelings of frustration or anger or unresolved issues from the past as well as the present.

Adults who were raised in abusive homes carry anger. Children who grow up in abusive homes learn violence as a means of

41

expressing and handling anger. They are at high risk to become abusers or get into relationships with abusers. They can carry anger or the fear of anger into their adulthood. If you don't understand how your past experiences affect you, you may recreate it. If you are abusive or are being abused, seek help.

Regardless of what kind of home you grow up in, you must express your feelings in healthy ways. If you don't, they will affect you in negative self-defeating or self-destructive ways. Excessive baggage prevents many people from going where they want to go, doing what they want to do, and being what they want to be.

DEALING WITH ANGER.

Here are several hints to help you deal with anger in appropriate ways.

✎ **Recognize your warning signs**. Ask yourself. Do you feel overwhelmed? Are you able to remain rational? Are you blaming someone else for your behavior? Are your reactions inappropriate?

✎ **Think before you react**. Don't personalize it. Question the importance of the situation. Ask yourself if there is another way to handle the problem.

✎ **If you are upset about something, take a time out**. Leave the room, go outside, or take a break to gain control.

✎ **Give yourself positive messages**. Eliminate negative ones.

✎ **Question your thinking and reaction**. Is there a better way to handle your anger? Could you have overreacted?

✎ **Have a two-way conversation with yourself**. Let the logical, rational part of your brain show you a different perspective.

✎ **Be empathic and understanding**. Respond the way you want someone to respond to you. Don't be quick to judge or criticize.

✎ **Do something physical**. Walk or jog around the block, do sit-ups/push-ups, jog in place. Take a swim, shoot hoops, use exercise equipment, go to the gym.

✎ **Identify your feelings**. Talk yourself through them. Think of the most responsible way to handle them. Question if there are other options. Talk to someone if you need to.

✎ **Use the ABCD approach**. (situation, belief, feelings and action, dispute)

A=Situation (look at the situation or problem objectively)

B=Belief (what is your perspective of the situation) Is it based on your bias belief? Are you objective? Is the situation or the problem your way of looking at things only?

C=Feelings & actions (how you think will determine how you feel and how you act) Think before you act.

D=Dispute (Question and challenge your reaction) Now respond to the situation.

FEAR

Fear is another natural, healthy feeling. The reality of fear is protection. If you are watching your child around the pool, your fear of the child drowning will keep you alert. This is a natural reaction to a normal fear. Carried fear however is panic, anxiety and paranoia. When fear is overwhelming and not realistic in nature, there is usually underlying fears that are not natural. Some people may experience fear of what others say and think about them, fear of abandonment, and fear of rejection or failure. These feelings may become

43

overwhelming. These types of fears affect other areas of their lives.

Dave experienced panic attacks around the same time his wife began working. In therapy, he realized he had overwhelming fears of his wife leaving him. He couldn't believe he felt that way. He had a good marriage. He was happy about her getting a job and felt less financial pressure because of it. They had even planned a vacation, which was canceled because of his panic attacks.

Dave said, "None of this makes sense to me. I know my wife isn't going to leave me, so why do I feel this way?"

I asked "Why do you think you feel that way?" He began to explore his true feelings. His fear triggered unconscious memories. When his mother went back to work, she had an affair and walked out on Dave and his dad. Dave was feeling like that 8 year old boy again. He was afraid he would be abandoned again. Dave is now 38 and has never seen his mother since her abandonment. You can see why the current situation would trigger such emotions, yet the emotions were not conscious nor did he even think he had any carried feelings from his childhood.

Everything that happens to you in life affects you. A simple rule of thumb is, if you overreact or are overwhelmed by something that seems minor or insignificant, question what else your reaction may be about. It may be something you haven't dealt with yet. It could be as simple as what happened yesterday. Remember, your past does not have to dictate your present or your future.

In Dave's case, he began to understand the impact his mother's leaving had on his life. He realized it still bothered him. He had learned to hide his feelings. He never talked about it, so he thought it didn't bother him. After he worked through his painful memories, he experienced feelings he had never allowed himself to have. He reexperienced the memory and, for the first time, expressed his true feelings of fear of abandonment, anger, hurt and sadness.

Dave began to see how fear affected other things in his life. Fear of changing jobs, fear of taking risks, and the list went on. The more he became aware, the more he could change. Now when he struggles with anxiety, he feels he knows what he is fighting and isn't so afraid. The best way to let go of baggage is to open it, see what's there, and choose what to get rid of or what to keep.

Having your feelings isn't always pleasant. However, it does free you from carrying baggage. When you ignore your feelings they can become unresolved issues. Then, any time you fear losing someone or something, you may become overwhelmed, overreact or experience anxiety or panic.

Angie never dealt with the loss of her father when she was young. She always struggled with abandonment issues. She was unhappy in her relationship, but afraid to confront her spouse for fear he would leave her. As she began to understand her feelings, she was able to confront her husband. They went to marriage counseling and made positive changes that enhanced their marriage. She overcame her fear of abandonment.

This would be a good time to journal any fears you think you may be carrying. Also journal times when you overreacted or felt overwhelmed by something you were concerned, worried or fearful about. Reread your entry later, and see if you learn anything about yourself.

SADNESS

Sadness is also a natural healthy feeling. The reality of sadness is growth. Allow yourself to express your sadness and deal with psychological pain through healthy means. Share with a friend, journal your feeling and thoughts, seek professional help if appropriate, attend a support or therapy group. If you allow yourself to grieve and cry, you are able to let go and move on with your life.

When you don't deal with sadness, you carry it and experience depression and despair. You become overly sensitive. When any loss or sadness occurs, or someone hurts your feelings, you become overwhelmed or overreact. Your unresolved sadness is being triggered. Look for feelings you have denied or what pain you are covering up. Deal with it the best way you can. Let it go, then move on.

My own father died one week before Thanksgiving. My hurt was very deep but I didn't want to feel the pain. I couldn't wait to buy a Christmas tree and put it up because in my mind I had convinced myself that once I celebrate Christmas everything would be okay. I had already lost my mother five years earlier and I couldn't bare to feel that kind of pain again. I felt so alone. I loved them both so dearly.

Everybody said it was too early to put up a real tree, but I insisted. It was the biggest and the best tree I ever had. After a few weeks my tree started to shed. Each day it got worse. Three days before Christmas my tree looked like the one in Charlie Brown's cartoon. I was angry. I yelled over minor things. I overreacted about everything. I almost pulled the tree down. I was screaming, "My tree is dead!" Then my feelings surfaced. I sobbed. It wasn't fair that my dad was dead. The tree triggered my true feelings. If you do not deal with feelings, you will stuff them in your baggage and carry them. Denying feelings holds you captive. You are not free to grow and move forward until you face them.

Does this trigger any feelings for you? Is there unresolved grief you've ignored because you didn't want to feel the pain? Now journal your feelings.

My grief:

_____
_____
_____

GUILT AND SHAME

Guilt and shame are also natural, healthy feelings. The reality of guilt and shame is accepting that we are fallible, human and not perfect. Guilt is about "doing." You break a value system or you do something wrong or make a mistake. When you do something wrong or make a mistake, you own it. You take responsibility for it. Shame is about "being." It is feeling that you are bad or you are a mistake. Carried shame is a feeling of worthlessness, inferiority, defectiveness, being dumb, stupid, damaged goods, or not as important or as good as someone else.

Tammy, a 36-year-old teacher was sexually abused when she was 6. She carried guilt and shame throughout her life. She believed she was defective and that even God couldn't love her. She hated herself. Tammy had flashbacks, memories and dreams of the abuse. She felt suicidal. At 26, she saw herself as a horrible, bad person who didn't deserve to live. At first, she was unable to separate what was done to her (a terrible, horrible act) from who she was (an innocent 6 year old child). However, in her 6 year old thinking, she incorporated these feelings and felt responsible for the abuse. When you are stuck in shame, you can't see the logic. Shame is the vulnerable feeling of embarrassment in front of others. Guilt is internal dissatisfaction as a result of what you have done. Tammy had done nothing wrong, but she questioned the shame she felt.

The painful dilemma of the adult who was victimized as a child and the adult who's trying to deal with the unresolved pain, is presented in this poem:

47

Logical (adult)	Emotional (child)
The sin I feel	If I'd only thought
is not my own	and didn't obey
I was a child	I'd be a much better person
HE was grown	than I feel today

HE committed the wrong	Yes, I was a child
I had no choice	But I did <u>decide</u>
I was only a child	That to HIS demands
with a small voice	I would abide

I <u>did</u> try to tell	Okay, so I told
of my heart filled with fear	But I didn't explain
In my own awkward way	Exactly why
Guess you didn't hear	I felt this pain

Am I feeling the child I can't bear to see?
Why does this child have to be me?

She really needs my help. Someday, somehow,
I guess I'll take the first step now.

The child in me is buried deep
but this child is mine to keep.

Becky Schwald-Brown   4/29/93

Tammy began to understand how her childhood trauma and pain affected her thinking and her life. The distinction between her past and present became clear, and she was able to make positive changes in her life. She left her past behind and moved on.

Feelings need to be expressed openly, appropriately, and honestly. When you constantly deny your feelings, you lose a part of yourself. After a while, your feelings become overwhelming and overpowering. You learn to stuff or freeze them. Whenever you overreact with your feelings, ask yourself if an old memory has the same feeling. Experience the feeling even if it is painful. Share your feelings with someone you trust so you don't have to stuff them again.

Journal any thoughts, memories or feelings that may have surfaced while reading Tammy's story. A few hours or even a few days later go back and read what you wrote. You will have more insight to your feelings. If you stuff your feelings too long, they will affect you physiologically, resulting in headaches, spasms, stomach problems or some other physical ailments. Your mind may forget temporarily, but your body will remind you.

My stuffed feelings

_____

_____

_____

If you have been the victim of any abuse, write your abuser a letter. (Don't mail it!) This is for you. In your adult thinking and logic, let them have it. Call them every name you can think of. Tell them off. Don't hold back. Empower yourself and let the secret be out. They were wrong. It is their sinful secret, not yours, give it back to them. When you are done, you can burn it, bury it, rip it up, or send it in a helium balloon to God and let Him take care of it. However you dispose of it, let it go. Any abuse can leave scars. The goal is to work through the feelings so you can let them go and move on with your life. Leave the past where it belongs, in the past, not in your present or future. If you need to tell about the abuse to the authorities, seek help first.

In a workshop by Michael T. Buck, Ph.D., he discussed how feelings locate in different parts of the body. Feelings become carried in the body when they are repressed, suppressed, and denied. In the head area, experiencing headaches can be feelings of loneliness, isolation, and abandonment. During the funerals of my mother and my father I experienced terrible headaches. Those feelings were so strong and so overwhelming that my body reacted to my emotional distress.

The throat can be the site of feelings of unresolved sadness and grief issues. Sometimes it feels like there is a lump in your throat and you have difficulty breathing or swallowing.

The chest can harbor feelings of unresolved fear. When a person is having a panic attack, they are overwhelmed with fear. They experience palpitations and their heart races. Understanding your feelings can help you deal with them and sometimes help to change your behavior or your reactions.

The stomach and gastrointestinal can be the area of feelings of unresolved anger. People that have ulcers and stomach problems may be carrying a lot of anger. WARNING: Of course, keep in mind that even if the physiological or medical problems are emotionally related, you still should see your doctor. Unresolved issues are not necessarily the only course of physiological ailments. There are many other reasons for those problems.

When your mind chooses to forget the memories, your body will remember the feelings. Your job is to listen to the body and deal with the feelings the best way you can. Of course, this does not mean that every time you have a headache or a stomach problem, you are experiencing abandonment or anger.

Feelings can be expressed in many healthy ways. You may express them by saying in words how you feel. (A good example is saying, "When you said that, I felt hurt.") You may share with a friend what is happening in your life and how you feel. You may express them physically, such as crying or making facial expressions that show how you feel instead of hiding or denying your feelings behind a mask of a smile or laughter.

Your actions will also show others how you feel. Do not be

passive. Don't act like a martyr or a victim. When appropriate, if you have something to say, say it. Don't pretend it doesn't bother you if it does.

Write anger letters, (<u>Don't</u> mail them. Mailing letters doesn't always give you the results you want. You may not be ready to deal with the reactions of others.) Write anything you want to say, don't hold back. Destroy the letters when you're done. Don't hold on to the past.

The most effective way to express feelings is openly, honestly, appropriately and assertively. Keep in mind that some people don't know how to respond when others show emotions. Remember, people's reactions are about them. Your reaction is about you. You have no control over other's behaviors or reactions. You can only control your reaction to them. Learn not to overreact or become overwhelmed by what you have no control over. As in the Serenity Prayer,

> **"Accept the things you cannot change and change the things you can."**

You have feelings about everything. You have feelings about people, places, things, situations, the past, the present, the future and yourself. If you have a difficult time identifying feelings, find a list of feelings or make one up with the help of a friend or counselor. If you stuff or freeze your feelings, you may find self-defeating ways of covering up the hurt and pain.

Feelings can seem overwhelming and overpowering. For people who have gone through traumatic childhoods, recovery is hard, but rewarding. It's painful remembering traumatic events. Ignoring and denying painful events eventually takes its toll. The goal is to deal with the feelings and move on. Do not get stuck in your feelings or your past.

Dealing with overwhelming and unresolved feelings is like the birthing process. It is different for everybody. For some, it can be long and painful. For others, it's quick. When it is over, it is over. The pain is forgotten.

In healing, you learn to let go of the past (get rid of the afterbirth so to speak). You choose to take responsibility for your life and move forward. Don't go through life holding an "I was a victim" or an "I am a survivor" sign. Understand your past, but don't become your past. Leave it behind.

If you were abused as a child, journal writing is helpful . You can write letters to the child within you, who was abused, hurt or abandoned. You can become for that little child a loving, nurturing parent.

You can write a **letting go** letter explaining how you are taking charge of your life and letting go of the past. Put the letter in a helium balloon. Go to a comfortable, safe place and let go of the balloon and your baggage.

There are many 12 Step support groups that can be helpful. The following can be found in the white pages of your telephone books. Alcoholics Anonymous (AA), Narcotics Anonymous (NA), Cocaine Anonymous (CA), Alanon, Sexual Abuse Anonymous, Adult Children of Alcoholics (ACA), Codependency Anonymous (Coda), Overeaters Anonymous (OA), and Emotions Anonymous (EA). The Rational Recovery support group is another alternative for alcoholics.

Support groups are fellowships of people coming together because of a similar problem. They will share their strengths, hopes and stories to help support you in recovery. If you are struggling with the loss of a loved one, find a grief group.

Learn from these groups. Take from them what is helpful and

what works for you. Throw out what doesn't fit. Experience your feelings but don't become stuck. Groups are to help you gain insight and give you tools to move on with your life. Stay as long as you need and leave when you are ready.

If you have been a victim of abuse you may want to understand how abuse affects you. Reading books about abuse, incest, shame, grief, codependency and addictions is helpful. Courses in self-esteem, eliminating self-defeating behavior, assertiveness, personal growth, communication and relationships are also helpful. (Most of these courses are offered at your local community colleges.)

If you feel overwhelmed by memories or feelings, it may be helpful to seek counseling. Painful memories and trauma are repressed as survival mechanisms. If you experience flashbacks, dreams and memories, you may feel overwhelmed. You are not going crazy or losing your mind. You are not alone. You need to deal with your feelings. The purpose of dealing with your past is not to get stuck there or to place blame. That will keep you angry and stuck. The purpose, is to understand your past so you don't repeat it.

Be like an archeologist. Dig enough so you know what was there, then learn from what you found. If you are not sure what you found, don't guess. Don't let someone else guess for you. Flashbacks can be deceiving. Don't overreact or analyze. Don't jump on any bandwagons. Find a good therapist who will help you find your own answers. Remember, archaeologists don't have to dig up every single bone to learn about their findings. Learn only what you have to learn, feel only what you have to feel.

Anyone can have unresolved issues. You do not have to grow up in a dysfunctional family or be a victim of abuse to have issues or problems. Don't become hypervigilant and analyze everything you say and do. Don't look for a hidden meaning to everything. Just be aware of your feelings and express them when appropriate. Control your feelings, don't let your feelings control you.

Take time now to journal any feelings that have come up since reading these chapters. In a day or two go back and reread what you wrote. You will have more insight.

Write statements of how you are going to eliminate your self defeating behaviors.

_____

_____

_____

To end this chapter, I would like to include a poem I think is especially appropriate. I do not know the author.

I WILL ALLOW MYSELF TO EXPERIENCE THE RICHNESS OF MY EMOTIONS

Am I scared to feel? Do I still block my emotions and deny my reactions to situations? To feel sometimes takes courage. Not to feel is to cut myself off from the joy of life as well as the pain.

Imagine what life would be like if I lost my sense of touch, I could not experience heat, cold, pleasure or pain. I would be totally numb to the information and the pleasures that touch brings. I do not want to anesthetize myself from life. Instead, I will allow my emotions to enrich my life and spirit. Today, I will allow my body to tell me what I'm feeling.

My emotions are a valuable resource to me and a gift that I gratefully accept.

Eliminating Your Self-Defeating Behaviors

Better Choices, Better Life

Chapter Four

How to Let Go of Guilt and Shame

- *Chapter Four* -

How to Let Go of Guilt and Shame

Some people carry too much guilt. Others try to dump their baggage of guilt on anyone who will take it. Healthy guilt makes you take responsibility for your feelings and your actions. It is not healthy to take on other peoples feelings or feel responsible for their actions. Unhealthy guilt can be debilitating and crippling. Too much guilt and shame makes you feel inferior or somehow defective.

Guilt is a feeling regarding a behavior. If you do something wrong, you feel bad. This is healthy guilt. Guilt is about "doing." You are human, not perfect. You will make mistakes. You must take responsibility for them. Most of you will not see your mistakes on CNN or on the front page of the newspaper. Most mistakes are minor. You do not need to beat yourself up. Own your behavior. Take responsibility for your behavior. Learn from your mistakes and move on. Do not take responsibility for another adult's thinking, feeling, actions or behaviors.

When you make a mistake, deal with it the best way you can. Take responsibility and face consequences. Work it out, make amends if appropriate and move on. When a harmless mistake is made, and no one is hurt by it, learn to say "Oh well. How important will this be a week from now?" Is there any benefit to holding on and obsessing over it? If there isn't, let it go. Don't put yourself down for being human!

I felt guilty when

_____

_____

_____

Shame is a feeling regarding your identity. You feel you are a mistake, defective, or worthless. Debilitating shame attacks your "being." Shame can be humiliating, overwhelming, and has intense feelings of uselessness and worthlessness. You wish you could hide or, sometimes, die.

I felt ashamed when

_____

_____

_____

In the book *Facing Shame,* Fossum and Mason define shame as an "inner sense of being completely diminished or insufficient as a person." In her book *Shame and Guilt: Masters of Disguise* Jane Middleton-Moz maintains "debilitating shame and guilt are at the root of all dysfunctions in families." Rokelle Lerner stated, "Shame is a form of family violence, it causes misery because it's socially accepted and it causes emotional scars. Shame occurs when our basic expectation of someone we love tells us we're bad or had done something wrong."

Families and relationships that carry shame have unrealistic rules. These rules, you "ought to" and you "should," are expected to be obeyed at all times, no exceptions. There is no room for mistakes. There is no distinction between the deed and the person. Good people make mistakes and sometime even breaks the rules. With shame, when you make a mistake the attack is usually aimed at the person's character. The belief is that the person is "stupid or bad." When a mistake is made there is shaming punishment because the belief is "you don't make mistakes, you should know better".

Be careful of the "shoulda's." If you let people, they will "should" on you. After a while, you "should" all over yourself. Eventually, you let everyone "should" all over you. Take charge of yourself and your life. Don't let people "should all over you anymore" and "stop shoulding all over yourself." You know what you should and should not do.

When you make a mistake, take responsibility for it. Ask yourself "How important will this be to me 6 months from now?" or "If the world ended tomorrow, how important is this today?" Ask yourself, "Whose shame is it, mine or the person who's trying to dump it on me?" Learn not to overreact to minor mistakes. Life will go on. When people around you overreact to a mistake, that's about them. Don't take it on. If you have to, have a two- way conversation with yourself. Talk it out until it makes sense to <u>you</u>.

Let go of your baggages of shame and don't take on those of other people. Stop all the unnecessary "shoulding." Remember these phrases when you start "shoulding" on yourself or when others start "shoulding" on you:

"People's reactions are about them, not me."

"My reactions are about me and I can change my reactions."

"I won't blame myself for the way someone else reacts."

"Just because (they) say it, doesn't mean it's true."

"Whose problem is it anyway, who's responsible?"

"I will not should on myself."

"I won't let anyone should on me."

"I have no control over other people or their problems."

"I can't change others, I can only change my reactions."

"I will not take responsibility for someone else's baggage."

"I have a right to live my life my way. If they don't like it that is their problem."

"I am responsible for the way I think, feel, react and behave."

"I am not responsible for the way others think, feel, react and behave."

This doesn't mean you can be hurtful and nasty to someone. Treat people the way you want to be treated. Don't carry other people's baggage, it will prevent you from doing things that are important to you. You already have enough baggage; learn how to recognize what's yours and what's not! Take responsibility for your actions, not others.

Some people are good at pushing buttons and trying to make you feel guilty. Keep in mind that they can't make you feel guilty unless you let them. People know what to say to get their needs met. If you expect to get your needs met, say what you want. (Most people flunk "Mind Reading 101.") State how you feel, what you want and what you don't want. Don't let others shame you because you think differently from them. Remember, you have a right to think differently. Just because you think different, doesn't make them right and you wrong. If others try to control you by telling you how you "should" think, feel or act, politely say "I won't should on you, please don't should on me."

Go through your baggage. Get rid of what doesn't belong to you. If it belongs to you, you are responsible. If it doesn't, you're not. It's like cleaning out a closet. If you store everybody else's things, there's no room for yours. Get rid of what doesn't fit anymore, what doesn't belong to you, and what you don't need or like. Decide what to keep and get rid of the rest.

Debilitating shame needs to be dumped. For some that means dumping on to anyone who will take it. For others, it means putting your arms out to take it. Either way is unhealthy and wrong. No one can dump baggage on you unless you let them. Don't blame others for dumping their baggage on you if you let them. Don't dump your baggage on others either.

Here are some dysfunctional strategies people use to hide feelings of shame:

✎ **CONTROLLING/OVER-CONTROLLING OTHERS**- Feels a need to control everyone and everything. They think they know what's best for everyone. They "should" on everyone. When you don't do things their way, they get angry and are very shaming.

✎ **BLAMING OTHERS** - Never takes responsibility for anything that goes wrong. Always has to find fault in someone or something If they make a mistake they immediately want to find fault in someone else for the mistake. Their reaction is, "Look at what you made me do!"

✎ **ACTING PERFECT/EXPECTING OTHERS TO BE PER-FECT** - Must always be right and demand perfection in others. Is intolerant of mistakes and is very critical and judgmental. No matter what you do, it is never good enough.

✎ **BEING INDIFFERENT** - Act like nothing bothers them. They act like they don't care. Inside they are afraid to show how they really feel. They appear hard and unloving and never express or share feelings.

✎ **COMPULSIVE** - They engage in self-defeating compulsive behaviors to keep busy and to avoid problems. They will not accept or admit responsibility for any problem.

Children who grow up in shame-based families believe they

are inferior or not as important as others. They learn their needs, wants and feelings are not okay. As adults, some experience depression, loneliness and low self-esteem. For some, their identity is consumed by trying to be what everybody else wants them to be. Many become a chameleon so they can change to please everyone. Some carry the faulty beliefs, dysfunctional thinking, and unrealistic expectations into their adult relationships. If you are carrying this shame, now is the time to get rid of it.

What or who's shame are you carrying?

_____

_____

Here are some helpful hints to deal with unhealthy shame:

✎ **Give affirmations to yourself**. Make positive, loving statements about yourself and your abilities. "I am lovable" "I am capable" "I can do it" "I am a good person" "I deserve to be treated with respect." If you don't believe these statements, say them until you do. Look in a mirror and convince yourself they're true. You may feel stupid at first but keep saying them until you believe them. Nothing will be real until you feel it.

✎ **Replace negative, dysfunctional tapes with positive healthy beliefs**. "I'm not selfish." "I have the right to say no." "If other people don't like me exercising my rights, that is their problem."

✎ **Learn to recognize the unhealthy beliefs and messages.** Image them as baggage and imagine yourself dumping them and walking away. Remember, just because they say it, doesn't mean it's true.

✎ **Set boundaries, set limits of what you will and will not accept from yourself and others**. Be consistent and stick to them. Be respectful of other peoples boundaries as well.

✎ **Remind yourself that you do have choices.** Misery is an option although not a healthy one. Don't allow others to mistreat you in any way. If you need help seek it. You don't have to be hypervigilant or aggressive. Stand up for yourself in an assertive manner when appropriate.

✎ **Take care of yourself and your needs.** Take time to play and have fun with the child part of you. Pamper yourself from time to time. Take pride in yourself. Begin to question "What do I want? What makes me happy?" Find a healthy balance.

✎ **Don't be a martyr. Don't be a victim.** Learn how to express your needs and stand up for them.

✎ **Think positively.** Find something positive even in something negative.

✎ **Stop looking at what you don't have or can't do, and look at what you can do.**

✎ **Accept the things you can't change.** You can change yourself, your reactions and your attitude. You can't change the way other people think or behave but you can choose if you want to be around them or listen to what they say.

✎ **Don't personalize everything people say or do.** People's reactions are about them, your reactions are about you.

✎ **Talk and share your feelings with a friend or get involved with a 12 Step support group.** You are not alone.

✎ **Identify and express feelings openly and appropriately.** Do not deny your feelings or your needs. Speak up for yourself. Let others know how you feel and what you need. Journal about your feelings.

✎ **Go through your shame, not around it.** If you need to, find an experienced, well recommended therapist to help you experience the feelings you have stuffed. You can't change what you don't see.

Under self-defeating behaviors you'll find baggage of unresolved issues or carried feelings. Remember, it could be yesterday's baggage. Don't over analyze everything in your life. Look at the problem and make a decision to do something about it. Take control and take responsibility.

It is uncomfortable when shame is exposed. When it is exposed, you may feel vulnerable. You will not appear on the news or on the front page of the newspaper. Don't get trapped in the "worry cycle," feeling overwhelmed, "shoulding all over yourself," carrying baggages of **"what if's"** and **"if I only's."** Hiding shame or your feelings will keep you stuck in self-defeating behaviors. Don't get trapped in the "blame cycle," blaming your past or others. As an adult, you are responsible for you, your feelings, and your actions. Your reaction is about you.

Some of you may need to go back and look at your family of origin. Look for the shaming messages, rules and beliefs in order to change them. Others may need to look at past relationships, friendships, workplaces or environments and see if you are carrying old baggage. Either way, it's cleaning your closet out. The goal is not to stay in the past, or blame anyone in the past. It is to understand the past and deal with the feelings, and then move on.

Make a list of all negative messages, faulty beliefs, etc., that you carry. Next, decide how you want to modify them and which ones you need to get rid of. Make a game plan of techniques you will use to help you eliminate those messages and behaviors.

List your negative messages, faulty beliefs, and unrealistic expectation:

_____

_____

Which ones need to be modified?

_____

_____

Which techniques will you use to change them:

_____

_____

You don't have to come from an abusive or shame based family to have shame. Shame is a feeling. There is nothing wrong with feeling ashamed when you do something wrong. It is excessive shame that is unhealthy, debilitating or crippling. Unhealthy shame becomes internalized. You carry it around and let it affect your life. You take everything personally.

You have to take responsibility for your life. Your thoughts, feelings, beliefs and behaviors may have originated from the past but you control your present and your future. If you blame your past or a person, you will carry your feelings and remain a victim. You may not be able to change your past, but you have control over how you want your past to effect you.

I would like to end this chapter with a poem from another unknown author.

I CAN HONOR MYSELF WITHOUT SEARCHING FOR APPROVAL

Today I no longer feel the desperate need to have everyone's approval. I will not submerge my real self to gain the approval of all. As an adult, I do not need to blindly seek the "OK" stamp from everyone, for everything.

I grew up with a criticizer in my consciousness that demanded perfection. I grew up trying to please everyone to obtain love. I reject that script today. I challenge the old belief that I will be rejected for being me.

Today I will relate to others with an inner conviction that I have worth. If this isn't natural for me, I will act as if it is. I will imagine myself as someone who feels self-worth and inner integrity. I will notice what it feels like and how I behave.

I will not go through life apologizing and being a self-defeating pleaser. Now that I am learning to love myself, I do not need to please everyone. Today, I approve of myself.

Chapter Four

Learning to Set Limits and Boundaries

- *Chapter Five* -

Learning to Set Limits and Boundaries

A boundary is a dividing line. It separates one area from another. It defines your personal space and your personal rights. You set boundaries to protect yourself from those who would violate your rights or space. Boundaries can be violated when others do not respect your rights.

A boundary is also a limit of how far you will go or how far you will let another go. It defines what you want and what you don't want. What behavior is acceptable to you and what is not. What you will tolerate and what you won't. It's about taking responsibility for yourself. A boundary defines yours needs, wants, feelings and actions. It's standing up for yourself and letting others know what they can, and cannot get away with.

You set boundaries because you have rights and you will not accept others violating them. Generally, you do not need to discuss or exercise those rights. Most people are respectful of them. Some are not. In those cases you must be assertive and make your boundaries very obvious. You do not have to hide behind a brick wall or wear a suit of armor for protection. Take responsibility. If you don't like something, change it.

Remember, you must respect yourself enough to say "I deserve respect; therefore, I will not let someone mistreat me or take advantage of me." No one will respect you if you don't respect yourself. Keep in mind, people can't mistreat you, unless you let them. You are a victim only if you let yourself be. Take charge of your life and your destiny. The destiny you arrive at in life depends on the roads you have chosen to take.

Boundaries are the limits you set and the rights that you assert. Here are some common types of boundaries:

✎ **Physical** - You have the right to decide who touches you or who gets close in your personal space. You have the right not to be abused.

✎ **Emotional** - You have the right to your feelings, the right to express them appropriately and the right not to have them invalidated.

✎ **Sexual** - You have the right to determine who, when, where and how to engage in intimate sexual relations. You have the right to say no, even to your spouse.

✎ **Intellectual** - You have the right to your own thoughts and opinions. You have the right to decide what is best for you. You have the right to change your mind and disagree with others.

✎ **Spiritual** - You have the right to be who you are and not have your spirit broken. You also have the right to determine a relationship with God or a higher power that you believe in.

Remember: Just as you have these rights, others do too.

Many adults who were abused as children believe they have no rights. Becoming adults does not necessarily change those beliefs. They have to be unlearned and replaced with new, positive beliefs if you don't want to stay a victim. You learned them, and you can choose to unlearn them. You have to be willing to stand up for yourself. Don't hesitate to seek professional help or attend a 12 Step support group if you need to.

Pia Melody described four kind of boundaries in her book *Facing Codependency*. They are intact, damaged, walled and none.

✎ **Intact** - You believe you have rights and exercise them. When someone violates those rights, you stand up for yourself and confront the person and the behavior. You do not stay with people who do not respect your rights.

✎ **Damaged** - You allow others to invade or violate your rights and boundaries most of the time. You have a difficult time standing up for yourself. You may stay in abusive or unhealthy relationships.

✎ **Walled** - You are afraid to let anyone in or close to you. You're afraid to be vulnerable. You put up an imaginary wall that keeps everyone out and also keeps you isolated and withdrawn. (This is common for those who have been hurt and are afraid of being hurt again.)

✎ **None** - You allow yourself to be a total victim. You let others mistreat or take advantage of you. You do not stand up for yourself or your property. You feel trapped and hopeless most of the time. You think, feel and therefore act like a victim. (This is common for those who are victims of domestic violence).

If you have walled or damaged boundaries, you need to re-pair them. You can't just take the wall down, you would be left with no boundaries. If you have no boundaries, you need to set them assertively. You must believe you have rights, and the right to be treated with respect. If someone has a problem with you standing up for your rights, that is their problem. Don't carry their baggage of beliefs. As you expect others to respect your rights and boundaries, you must also respect the rights and boundaries of others.

Setting boundaries is nothing more than setting limits. It's taking responsibility for how you choose to live your life. You don't set boundaries to change others. Some people will never change or be respectful of your rights. It is your choice if you want to be around people like that. If you must be around them, limit your time. Continue to be assertive. Let them know how you feel. Don't tolerate abuse. Walk away from them if you have to. Be consistent. Follow through with what you say.

Ernie Larson in his book *Life Beyond Addiction: Understanding the Basics of Recovery* states:

> **"As you perceive it, you define it, as you define it, you set your limits."**

If your perception is that you are a worthwhile person who deserves respect, you will not tolerate abuse from others. If your perception is that you are defective, unlovable or worthless, you define yourself as deserving abusive behavior. When you do not set limits to stop abuse, you enable the abuser to continue the behavior and you further victimize yourself. You do not always have control over what happens to you or what someone else does. You do, however, have control over how you handle it.

Here are some helpful hints to repair or rebuild boundaries:

1. Do not take what everybody else says personally. People's reactions are about them. There are many people that take out their anger on other people. Don't personalize that, it's not about you. <u>Your</u> reaction is about you.

2. Stop overusing defense mechanisms; **denial,** ignoring the reality of the problem; **minimizing,** making light of the problem; **rationalizing,** making excuses and justifying, and **intellectualizing,** thinking instead of feeling, using intellect and explanations to cover feelings.

3. Set limits. Stop all forms of abusive behavior. Do not tolerate inappropriate behavior or abusive remarks. Confront the person and the behavior. Leave if you are at risk and get help.

4. Be honest with yourself. Do not lie to yourself. Admit the problem and begin to deal with it. Do not avoid or dissociate. The problem will not go away on it's own.

5. Keep things outside your boundary until you are ready to deal with them. Take time outs as needed. Call a friend for an objective point of view. Think it through before you act on it. Learn to say "dismiss" to yourself and let it go.

6. Begin changing old dysfunctional beliefs. List beliefs, messages, rules and thoughts that cause you pain and replace them with functional healthy affirmations and beliefs.

7. Experience feelings. Allow yourself to feel and experience the feelings. Do not stuff or freeze them. Release them in healthy ways, for example, crying, sharing with a friend, working out, going to a support group. You need to stand up for yourself and be able to take risks by expressing your feelings.

8. Focus on what you can change and what you have control over. Stop trying to change others. You have no control over others. You only have control over how you react to them.

9. Sort through your baggage and get rid of what doesn't belong or fit. Learn to say no when you need to. Don't take on another person's anger, hurt or guilt. Be compassionate and understanding but not to the point where it damages you in the process.

If you have never set boundaries before, people will not react the way you'd like them to. They may get angry or feel hurt. Don't feel guilty. This does not mean you are responsible for their feelings. Be respectful and treat them the way you would like to be treated, but stand up for yourself. Don't meet their needs while ignoring your own. This does not mean you don't care about others. There is nothing wrong with going out of your way or helping people. Just find a healthy balance.

You do not need to become self-centered or selfish. Learn when to draw the line. Take care of yourself first. When flying in an airplane, you are instructed how to use the oxygen mask in case of an emergency. They tell you if you are traveling with a small child to place the mask on yourself first then on the child. Well, is that selfish or does the airline not like kids? Obviously, you know you can't help the child if you don't help yourself first. If the people in your environment have problems adjusting to your rights and boundaries, let them deal with it.

In the book *Beyond Codependency*, Melody Beattie gives tips for setting boundaries. Here are a few taken directly from that book:

"1. When we identify that we need to set a limit with someone, do it clearly preferably without anger, and in as few words as possible.

2. We cannot simultaneously set a boundary and take care of another person's feelings.

3. We'll set boundaries when we're ready, and not a minute sooner."

Setting boundaries is a learning experience; sometimes it

works, sometimes it doesn't. The key is, don't give up when something doesn't work. Learn from it and learn why it doesn't work. Find out what you have to do to make it work.

Unfortunately, not everyone will respect your boundaries. Not everyone will believe you'll follow through with the boundaries you have set. Many will test you. Believe you have rights. Be consistent. Exercise your rights. Don't back down. Eventually others will learn that you won't allow those limits to be pushed anymore.

You are the only one who can control the limits you have set. Unless of course, you are willing to give control up to someone else. Setting boundaries is taking care of yourself. When people respect you, there is no need to set boundaries. It's an automatic mutual unspoken respect. There are, however, people who will not respect them. Set boundaries with them, regardless of their reactions.

Learn to listen to yourself. Respect others but respect yourself too. Know your rights and exercise them. When you respect yourself, others will respect you. If they don't, respect yourself enough not to allow them to "should" on you. Don't give them the power to control you. Empower yourself.

Boundaries are a personal issue. You have the right to let some people come close and to keep others at a distance. You have the right to stand up for yourself. You have the right to confront people when they do not respect you or your boundaries. How they react, of course, is about them. If they will not respect you, ask yourself, "Why am I still putting up with it?"

Having boundaries indicates having a healthy sense of self. You need to know who you are, what you want, and what you don't want. You respect others and you expect them to respect you. You believe you have the right to be respected and accepted for yourself. It is your responsibility to set your boundaries. No one will do it for you. You will have no one to blame but yourself if you don't stand up for your rights, feelings, beliefs and choices.

Without boundaries, others will control your life. Remember, no one can control your life unless you let them. You don't have the power to change other people. You do have the power to change yourself. You will not always feel good after you set boundaries. You may feel guilty. That's normal. But be consistent. Follow through with what you say. Don't feel guilty for treating yourself with respect.

What kind of boundaries do I have? _____

Who do I have the hardest time setting boundaries with?

_____

What faulty beliefs do I have to eliminate to have intact boundaries?

_____

_____

_____

I need more, or better boundaries in these areas, with these people.

_____

_____

_____

I would like to end this chapter with this poem. Author unknown.

I AM IN CHARGE OF MY LIFE,
I CHOOSE TO EXPERIENCE LOVE & HARMONY

I am the one in charge of my every experience. It is my lifelong responsibility to take charge of all that I am. I do this with delightful anticipation, knowing that I possess the power and strength to create a healthy existence.

The messages that I give myself today will be clear, positive and definite. I will be sure that these messages are received by putting them into action.

Critical or judgmental voices play no part in my thinking and I listen to my inner wisdom. I will not permit any voice, within or without, to sway me from my chosen path of health, love and wholeness.

I am the Chairperson of my Board. I am in charge of my life. I write my own agenda. Inner dissension and disruption will be squelched, as I conduct my life in balance and harmony.

Chapter Six

Building and Recreating Self-Esteem

- *Chapter Six* -

Building and Recreating Self-Esteem

What is self esteem? According to L.S. Barksdale, in his book *Building Self Esteem*, it is "accepting yourself for who you are and believing that you are a worthwhile person who is deserving of love and respect from others." In it's simplest form, it is how you feel about yourself.

Many people ask, If you've never had self-esteem, can you get it? If your self esteem is damaged, can it be rebuilt? Can you raise your self-esteem? The answer to the above questions is yes. Learning to believe in yourself and feeling good about yourself is a learning experience.

L.S. Barksdale discussed two basic beliefs of self-esteem. The first is that "no one is born with a sense of being an individual nor with a sense of self-esteem." His second principle is "self esteem is a process of learning to like oneself through feedback and positive life experiences." If the feedback in our environment is negative, critical and abusive, then we perceive ourselves as not worthy or deserving or respect.

The "IALAC" is an imaginary sign that means **I A**m **L**ovable **A**nd **C**apable. When the feedback in your life is negative or abusive, the sign becomes tarnished or erased. If you don't feel lovable and capable, you must work on changing the negative and faulty messages you've carried. Replace them with healthy ones.

Here are some examples of hurtful and abusive messages "You're stupid" "What's the matter with you?" "Can't you do anything right?" "You're no good." "You're such a loser." "You're a sicko." "You're crazy." "You can't make it alone." When you are told often enough that you are no good or unloved, you begin to believe it.

When you do not feel good about yourself, your self-esteem decreases. This is a time when you are a high risk to engage in self-defeating, compulsive behaviors. The behavior covers up the shame and feelings of inferiority. That is why you must set boundaries and stop all forms of abuse.

A humanistic psychologist, Abraham Maslow (1908-1970), formulated a theory on the Hierarchy of Needs. He theorized that when all your basic and emotional needs are met, you will become self-actualized (the ability to achieve your full potential). According to Maslow, the basic needs (physical, safety and security) must be satisfied before the emotional needs (love, belonging, esteem and self-esteem) can be met.

Your self-esteem gets damaged when you are in an abusive or dysfunctional relationship. Some stay in these relationships to get their basic needs met. However, your self-worth, self-esteem, and identity are damaged by the abuse. If your self-esteem has been damaged by abuse, seek help. You need to leave if the abuse doesn't stop.

In the introduction of their book *Chicken Soup For The Soul* (which is a wonderful book that I highly recommend), Jack Canfield and Mark Victor Hansen wrote:

"We know everything we need to know to end the needless emotional suffering that many people currently experience. High self-esteem and personal effectiveness is available to anyone willing to take the time to pursue it."

In order to build or rebuild self esteem you must work on your attitude. What you think is what you feel. What you feel is the way you treat yourself and others. It is also how you let others treat you. If you think you can't stand up for yourself or say no, you will feel uncomfortable and feel guilty when you do. If you feel uncomfortable and guilty, you will let others mistreat you and take advantage of you.

Do you ever notice that some people are never bothered, bullied or dumped on by others. Is there someone that you are thinking about whom you could say, "She'd never let them get away with that" or "They would never say or do that to her?" They even respect that person and accept her for who she is. What makes the difference? Is that person really better than you are? No! She just don't let other people control the way she thinks, feels, or acts.

People who are assertive and set boundaries don't allow others to take advantage of them. They don't allow people to dump their baggage on them either. Some people will not like it when you stand up for yourself or disagree with them, but they know they can't control you. If they can control you, they won't accept "NO" because they know you will change your mind if they are persistent. You must be consistent and follow through.

It's the "Vegas Principle." If you play a slot machine and nothing comes out, after awhile you look to another machine to give you what you want. If something comes out, you keep playing. When you consistently stand up for yourself and don't give in, people go elsewhere to dump their baggage. They may come back and try again. Be consistent and follow through with what you say. If you are not consistent, they'll keep trying because they think they may win again.

Life is not the lottery, it's **reality.** They can't win if you don't play." The only people that can control you are the ones you let control you. If you don't want others to control your life, believe in yourself and feel good about yourself. Take charge of your life. Don't control others and don't let others control you. If you do, you will be miserable, you have choices. Misery is optional.

I have poor self-esteem about _____
_____
What am I going to do to increase my self-esteem._____
_____

The first concept in having a sound self esteem is "Respect."

R - Respect yourself and others. Don't allow others to mistreat or take advantage of you. If you don't respect yourself, your feelings, your thoughts or your opinions, no one else will.

E - Express your feelings openly and appropriately. Do not stuff, deny or ignore how you feel about things. Be honest about your feelings. Take responsibility for your feelings. Don't take responsibility for how someone else feels or how they react. Don't let your feelings overwhelm or control you.

S - Stand up for yourself. Don't allow others to control you or tell you how to live your life. If it doesn't feel right, don't do it. This does not mean you have to confront everyone and everything at all times. Learn to say "No."

P - Positive Attitude and Positive Thinking. Take negative thoughts and turn them into positive ones. If you feel overwhelmed, ask yourself "What's the worst that could happen and how important will this be six months from now?" Turn obstacles into stepping stones to move forward. Don't worry, Be happy.

E - Eliminate all dysfunctional beliefs, tapes, messages and irrational thoughts. Change them into healthy, functional beliefs. Remember, it's like cleaning out a closet. Get rid of what doesn't fit or doesn't make you feel good and get rid of anything that doesn't belong to you.

C - Control your happiness. Make good choices. Take Charge. Don't blame your past or others for your unhappiness. Control your destiny. If you make poor choices or make mistakes, own it, deal with it, and move on. Your choices and decisions have consequences. Choose the direction of your life wisely.

T - Throw away all excessive baggage. Let go of unresolved issues and painful experiences or relationships. Don't let something negative or painful from your past determine your future. Don't hold on to anger or resentment. Don't hold grudges. Treating yourself with respect is important to strengthening self-esteem. In order to keep a sound self esteem you must work at it.

Here are some simple "Don'ts" to keep in mind:

1. **Don't be critical of yourself or others.**
2. **Don't catastrophize or make mountains out of molehills.**
3. **Don't overreact. Take a step back and think first.**
4. **Don't hold on to resentments. Don't stay angry.**
5. **Don't play the role of the victim or the martyr.**
6. **Don't take responsibility for other peoples' baggage.**
7. **Don't take on other people's feelings.**
8. **Don't let others control your thoughts, feelings or life.**
9. **Don't expect things to be perfect. Things go wrong.**
10. **Don't always put others needs and feelings above yours.**
11. **Don't be pessimistic. Learn to look on the bright side.**

12. Don't be negative. Look for the positive.

13. Don't take things so seriously. Have a good sense of humor.

Remember, if you don't treat yourself with respect, no one else will. If you are still struggling with how you feel about yourself, practice making positive, affirmation statements:

"I am a worthwhile person deserving of respect."

"I am in charge of my life. I choose my destiny."

"I am just as good and just as important as anyone else."

People with low self-esteem tend to worry what other people think. In contrast, people with high self-esteem don't determine who they are by the opinions of others. People with low self-esteem always want everyone to like them. They are people pleasers. People with high self-esteem accept that not everyone will like them. They acknowledge that there are some people you can't please no matter what you do. They accept the fact that reactions of other people are about other people, not themselves. They don't personalize how people respond or react to them.

As you can see, attitude has a lot to do with one's self-esteem. The way you think determines how you feel. The way you feel determines how you act. Make a list of beliefs and thoughts that determine how you feel and how you act. As you go through the list, get rid of the beliefs or thoughts that keep you trapped in low self-esteem.

What beliefs and thoughts keep me trapped in low self-esteem?

_____

Here are some helpful hints to build self-esteem:

1. Surround yourself with people that respect you, your

thoughts, your opinions, your feelings and your rights.
Be with pepople you respect.

2. Be kind and gentle to yourself. Forgive yourself for your mistakes. Ask for forgiveness when appropriate.

3. Somethings are clearly about right and wrong. You know the difference. Realize that not everything is about right or wrong. Sometimes things or ways of doing things are just different.

4. Give yourself credit and praise when you do a good job or accomplish something. Don't be critical.

5. Pamper yourself. Treat yourself to something special.

6. Make choices and decisions based on your needs, wants and desires, not someone else's. This does not mean to become self-centered or uncaring. Find a balance.

7. Learn to accept compliments graciously. Just say, "Thank you."

8. Have a positive outlook and attitude in everything you do. Look for the light at the end of the tunnel and always look for the rainbow after the storm.

9. When things don't go the way they were planned, accept it as part of life and don't over react to it. Say "Oh well." Remember, you can't use "Oh well" as a copout in more serious problems. Know the difference.

10. Let go of your worries, fears and baggage. Be free to be YOU. Have faith in yourself and God. Remember, God will not abandon you. He will carry you in your time of need.

11. "Dismiss" unhealthy thoughts or beliefs. Take control over your thoughts and feelings instead of letting them control you.

12. Smile more. Make a conscious effort to be happy.

13. Take charge of the direction of your life. Live by good values, morals, and respect yourself. Find a balance.

Remember, your happiness is controlled by you. Don't let others determine how you feel about yourself. Most of them don't know who you are inside. Their opinion is just their opinion. Opinions are like noses, everybody has one. Yours is unique for you.

I would like to end this chapter with the Poem "The Ugly Flower"

THE UGLY FLOWER
by Dan Goodale

The ugly flower wept, the tear did stream down to the sand,

and it wondered why it had been put alone upon the land,

so different from all the rest, ridiculed and lost,

and pondered for the evil deed that carried such a cost.

Immersed in sorrow so ashamed, it hid itself from light,

and hoped for death to ease the pain and end its hopeless plight.

Yet still it lingered, with no care, for life, love and living.

"For I" it thought, have nothing worth the taking or the giving.

The other flowers laughed and jeered at such an ugly one,

no yellow petals spread to grasp for soothing rays of sun,

a large ungainly mass of red with no redeeming grace,

and petals cupped to hide from view a most unwholesome face,

and quite distasteful to the rest an odor did appear,

quite nauseating in itself and harmful they did fear,

so doubling animosity they threatened jeered and taunted,

and made for that poor ugly flower a life quite devil-haunted.

And then one day a tractor came to till the fertile land,

and screaming loudly, flower by flower did slip beneath the sand.

So foot by foot, the tractor crept closer to that flower

and joyfully the flower did praise the long awaited hour.

The tractor stopped, a man did slip down quietly to stare,

and soon he started digging round that flower with great care,

transplanting it with gentle hands a question he did pose,

how among these dandelions, had there come to be a rose.

Eliminating Your Self-Defeating Behaviors

Better Choices, Better Life

Chapter Seven

Communicating in Assertive Ways

- *Chapter Seven* -

Communicating in Assertive Ways

If you have dumped your baggage, dealt with unresolved feelings and issues and set boundaries, why do people still act the way they do? Remember, people's reactions are about them. Your reactions are about you. Therefore, changing you doesn't change anyone else. It may change how they respond to you. Just because you're assertive and set healthy boundaries doesn't mean others will respect them. You set them to take care of yourself. When you set boundaries, you must communicate them in an assertive way. Assertiveness is not synonymous with aggression.

Aggression is taking care of yourself without care or concern of others. You don't care what you do to others, as long as you get what you want. Some examples of aggressive communication are yelling, name calling, blaming and intimidation. Aggressive people usually do not take responsibility for their words or actions. They blame everyone else for them, examples are "you made me do that" or "if you didn't do that I wouldn't have done that," "it's your fault.") Keep in mind, just because they say it, doesn't mean it's true.

Some people will use intimidation. They may threaten verbally or physically when they don't get what they want. They are manipulative and controlling. If you give in to prevent an outburst, they become more aggressive.

Assertiveness is taking care of yourself but not at another's expense. You are sensitive to others, but not at the risk of not taking care of yourself or being manipulated. You know when to draw the line and when to say no. You set boundaries. You let others know what is acceptable and what is not. Your approach is a respectful one. If the other person doesn't respect your boundaries, you "stick to your guns." You remain consistent and assertive.

An example of being assertive is, dealing with the person directly. You own your own feelings "I am angry." You're responsible for how you feel. You don't blame others for your feelings. You don't say, "You made me angry." Instead, you make "I" statements. "I don't appreciate what you said" or "I am not willing to do that," "I am upset with you." Keep in mind, though you are assertive and express your feelings openly, appropriately, and honestly, it will not guarantee that all others will understand and be accepting.

Being assertive is not about changing others. Assertiveness is taking care of yourself. Assertive communication is expressing yourself openly and respectfully. To be assertive is to respect yourself and others. You don't take responsibility for other peoples feelings or actions. This doesn't mean you don't care. You don't let someone else make you feel guilty about how they think or feel.

Have you tried being assertive or when you asserted yourself someone tried to make you feel guilty for getting your needs met? Remember, no one can make you feel guilty but yourself. When you don't give in to what others want, they may try to manipulate you. I call that the "tennis game." The goal of tennis is to win. A player has a better chance of winning if he finds the opponent's weakness and serves the ball there. So in your life, someone serves. You say "I don't want to play." Your opponent gets angry and tries to make you feel guilty with the next serve. When you don't take the "serve/guilt," they try again. The game goes back and forth using guilt, intimidation, manipulation, insensitive remarks, and anger until you either "play the game" or the game ends. Some people are pros at this game. Remember, "They can't win if you don't play."

When some people don't get their way, they look into their "bag of tricks" to find what will work.

Let's role play an example of a friend wanting you to babysit so she can go away for the weekend with friends.

Ann   "I need you to babysit this weekend."

Sue   "I'm sorry I can't, I have plans."

Ann   "Can't you change them?" (Ignoring your needs completely.)

Sue   "No."

Ann   "What are they? This is so important to me." (Concerned about herself only, wanting to change your mind.)

Sue   "I'm meeting with friends Saturday and I have to study and take care of things on Sunday."

Ann   "Can't you meet your friends another time? Besides, the baby wouldn't be any trouble while you study." (Control)

Sue   "No, I'm sorry. Not this time."

Ann   "I have always babysat for you when you needed me." (Guilt)

Sue   "You're right and I appreciate that. I've babysat for you, too, but I can't this weekend." (Consistent/assertive).

Ann   "I can't believe you won't do this for me. Now I lose my deposit and a chance to get away. You know how stressed I've been." (Manipulation and giving you baggage of guilt and responsibility for her losing her deposit and sanity).

Sue   "I'm sorry, not this weekend." (Consistent/assertive).

Ann   "Forget it, you just think of yourself. You are so selfish sometimes." (Anger, reverts to name calling as a final chance to see if you will change your mind).

The above example is common. Also, keep in mind, just because someone calls you something (selfish) doesn't mean it's true.

For example, Ann called Sue selfish because she was angry and wasn't getting her needs met. It was Ann who was selfish for thinking only of herself and trying to make Sue feel guilty. She was not respecting Sue's right to say no. If you are not consistent, people will continue to play the tennis game until you give in. They can't win if you don't play.

Remember the "Vegas principle," if you let others win every once in awhile, they continue to play until they win again. Be consistent. Even in the "tennis game," if they pick up their ball and refuse to "play" anymore, that's not a bad thing. The game playing ends. If you lose the friendship, I assure you it wasn't a healthy one based on respect. It was a relationship based on control and manipulation, where there is always a winner and a loser.

There's nothing wrong with helping others and even sometimes changing your plans to accommodate others, if you want to. However, it should not be done because of guilt, manipulation or game playing. It should be by your choice because you feel it's the right thing to do. When the element of choice is taken from you, you feel powerless, manipulated, controlled. You feel victimized. Don't render yourself powerless to others. Don't give up your right to choose what you want to do.

Being assertive is being consistent. After a while, others will know what they can and cannot get away with. Most people respect you when you respect yourself. We are creatures of habit. If we know we can get things from others through certain means, we do whatever we have to, to get what we need.

Passive is a form of ineffective communication. You play the role of the victim or the martyr. You stuff your feelings. You do things you don't want to do. You resent others because you believe they make you do things you don't want to do. You feel people take advantage of you and don't appreciate you. You feel powerless over your life. You believe you can't stand up for yourself because no one will let you. If this is your belief, you will feel like a victim and act like one. Take charge of your feelings, thoughts, and direction of your lift.

Passive people are never taken seriously when they say "no." They are generally inconsistent and usually give in to others. They do not express their feelings, thoughts or needs. They feel responsible for other people's feelings and needs. They are people pleasers. They do what others want, therefore, they feel cheated. They tend to be depressed, unhappy people. They have a negative, pessimistic outlook about life. They are unable to see the light at the end of the tunnel in situations. They usually are afraid to "rock the boat."

Passive aggressive communication is also ineffective. Passive aggressive people let you know how they feel through body language or their actions. They don't express their feelings.

Here are some examples of passive aggressive behavior:

1. **Walks away angry or hurt but doesn't say anything.**
2. **Talks behind someone's back.**
3. **Never confronts or discusss what is bothering himwith the person directly.**
4. **Says one thing and does another.**
5. **Doesn't follow through on commitments.**
6. **Procrastinates.**
7. **Blames everyone and everything.**
8. **Doesn't take responsibility for their actions.**

Just because someone blames you for something, doesn't make them right and you wrong. You have rights, exercise them.

Some basic rights are:

. **To think, feel and act for yourself.**

. **To have your own opinions.**

. **To be treated with respect.**

. **To change your mind.**

. **To stand up for yourself.**

. **To say "No" when you don't want to do something.**

. **To make mistakes.**

. **To ask for what you want or need.**

. **To feel the way you do and express yourself without being put down.**

. **Not to be mistreated or abused in anyway.**

. **To be happy.**

Although you do not have to be hypervigilant about your rights, you must be willing to stand up for them when they are in jeopardy. Remember, the same rights you have, others have too. Find a balance. Treat yourself and others with equal respect. If you don't assert your rights, no one will do it for you.

People I need to be more assertive with: _____

_____

Situations I need to be more assertive about:

_____

_____

I am too aggressive about:

_____

_____

I am too passive about:

_____

_____

I am too passive/aggressive about: _____

_____

I'd like to end with the following poem. Author unknown.

THE PERSON IN THE GLASS

When you get what you want in your struggle for self,
and the world makes you king or queen for a day,
just go to a mirror and look at yourself,
and see what that person has to say
for it isn't your father, mother, husband or wife
whose judgment upon you must pass,
the person whose verdict counts most in your life
is the one staring back from the glass
some people might think you're a straight-shooting chum,
and call you a wonderful gal or guy
but the person in the glass says you're only a bum
If you can't look him straight in the eye.
You're the person to please, never mind all the rest,
for you'll be with you clear up to the end
and you've passed your most dangerous, difficult test
If the person in the glass is your friend
You may fool the whole world down the pathway of years,
and get pats on the back as you pass
but your final reward will be heartaches and tears
if you cheated the person in the glass.

Chapter Eight

Taking Control of Your Attitude and How You Think

- Chapter Eight -

Taking Control of Your Attitude and How You Think

Your thoughts, beliefs and feelings influence your moods and the way you think and act. Your environment, lifestyle, and life experiences also influence you. If your environment is stressful, your life becomes stressful. When you are anxious and worried all the time, you overreact to things. You may become anxious over change, and panic when you feel you have little or no control.

It is not by mistake a person thinks they have to be perfect in everything they do. Our society places importance on performance and possessions. When things don't go as planned, you may become overwhelmed or depressed. Too much stress or obsessive thinking can cause problems and affect day to day functioning.

Once a person becomes overwhelmed with thoughts, feelings and their life in general, they engage in faulty, negative thinking. This can have damaging effects. Your thoughts become obsessive and you feel trapped in your thinking. This is a time when you are a high risk for depression or anxiety.

Rita came into therapy after the birth of her first child. She was depressed. She believed it was just postpartum depression. She also experienced anxiety. She had a panic attack the day before her first session.

She was complaining of little or no energy, no motivation, fatigue, stomach upset, dizziness, sweats, palpitations and heart racing. She was sleeping 12 hours a day. She was nervous, anxious, panicky and depressed. She was crying, arguing with husband, and avoiding taking care of the baby. She cried and said, "I'm not a good mother. My husband is going to want to divorce me. My family would be better off without me."

Rita felt overwhelmed. Her thoughts were not logical or rational in proportion to the changes in her life. Her reactions and behaviors were influenced by her mood, her thoughts and her feelings. They impacted her physically and emotionally. As she challenged her faulty beliefs, she was able to change them. She then dealt with her new role and a new baby in a more healthy way.

She also began to express her feelings instead of stuffing them. Her husband was always around when her emotional volcano blew. She was able to recognize that she was taking things out on him. She took responsibility and changed that. Her reactions were about her. As she took control of her feelings and actions, her anxiety and depression lessened.

Think of an easy 1-2-3 approach:

1. What do I think about the situation? What's my attitude? What are my beliefs? What faulty thoughts surface?

2. How do I feel about the situations? What feelings are surfacing and what physiological changes are occuring?

3. What am I going to do about the situation?

Using the above 1-2-3 approach, you can see Rita's faulty beliefs. She was thinking she was a bad mother and her husband would want a divorce. She felt overwhelmed, scared, anxious and depressed. Once you know why you do what you do, you have to take responsibility to change what is wrong. In Rita's case, her thinking was wrong. As she worked through her feelings and challenged her faulty thinking, she was then able to handle the problem and the situation more appropriately.

As you begin to understand your thinking, feelings, moods and behaviors, you get a better understanding of why you behave and react the way you do. You are responsible for your actions. You have the ability to eliminate the faulty thinking and change inappropriate or self-defeating behavior. You can then target behaviors, thoughts, moods or feelings and work on improving your attitude and behavior.

Some of this will be easy and exciting. Some will be more difficult to recognize and change. Some may be painful and trigger unresolved issues and feelings. If you need help, don't hesitate to seek it. What seems easy for one person may be hard for another. It doesn't make one person better than another, just different.

Everyone has different life experiences and different environments. Who we are has been influenced by many people, places, things and experiences. Even under the worse circumstances, you can make change occur and have a better life.

How you think will determine how you behave. Your thoughts can influence your physiological state. If you were home alone, heard a noise and saw someone trying to break in, wouldn't you have a physical reaction? You bet you would! Your heart might pound and race, your breathing might become erratic. Your body would react to your emotion.

Your thoughts can also influence your emotional state. In the above example you would have felt frightened. Your thoughts would trigger other thoughts. Your fear would trigger other fears. You might become overwhelmed. People react differently. In the above example there may be many reactions. The reactions may range from dialing 911, hiding in a closet or getting a weapon, to running out the back door.

As Henry Ford once said:

> **"Whether you think you can or whether you think you can't, either way, you're right."**

It's obvious that the way you think has a big impact on who you are. It affects how you behave, react and feel, and what you do. Your reactions are about you. You must take responsibility for your thinking and actions. Recognize which thoughts are rational, logical and healthy, and which ones are not. Question your thinking and challenge faulty beliefs. Let go of beliefs that don't fit or belong to you. Be less critical of yourself and others. As you begin to make changes in your thoughts and attitudes, your reactions and behaviors change too.

Whenever Rita became overwhelmed she reverted to her faulty thinking. She remembers her 1-2-3 approach and she was able to handle the situation better. She admitted that while we worked on this example her childhood abandonment issues of her father were triggered. Although I validated her feelings regarding her father abandoning her and her mother. I also reminded her, that was about her mother and father, not her and her husband. It helped put things in the present and in better perspective.

We also challenged her faulty beliefs of "not being able to do ANYTHING right. She became more aware that she thinks and speaks in extremes such as ALWAYS, NEVER, EVERYTHING, ALL THE TIME. The more she was aware, the more insightful of her own attitude, thoughts, feelings and actions she became. It also helped keep the past separate from the present.

Rita was also able to see that thinking her husband wanted a divorce was irrational and faulty. Especially after she and her husband sat down at talked. When she reevaluated her thinking, she became aware that she causes her own stress, anxiety and depression. After she talked with her husband, she rated her depression, anxiety and anger at 0%.

Awareness is the beginning. You must be willing to challenge your faulty thinking. The more insightful you become about yourself, the more control you have over your life.

If you don't like the direction your life is going, do something about it. You are only stuck if you let yourself be. If you can't do it alone, reach out and get help. You do not always have control over what happens in your life, but you do have control over how you deal with it. It begins with your attitude.

I would like to end the chapter with Charles Swindoll's perception on attitude.

ATTITUDE

"The longer I live, the more I realize the impact of attitude on life. Attitude, to me is more important than facts. It is more important than the past, than education, than money, than circumstances, than failures, than successes, than what other people think or say or do. It is more important than appearance, giftedness or skill. It will make or break a company, a church, a home. The remarkable thing is we have a choice everyday regarding the attitude we will embrace for that day. We cannot change our past, we cannot change the fact that people will act in a certain way. We cannot change the inevitable. The only thing we can do is play on the one string we have, and that is our attitude. I am convinced that life is 10% what happens to me and 90% how I react to it. And so it is with you, we are in charge of our attitudes."

Better Choices, Better Life

Chapter Nine

Healthy vs. Unhealthy Relationships

- *Chapter Nine* -

Healthy vs. Unhealthy Relationships

Relationships are part of everyday life. How you react to other people has a big impact on how others react and treat you. If you expect very little from your relationship, that's what you'll get. If you expect too much from your relationship, you'll be disappointed. Find a healthy balance.

Honesty, respect, love, commitment and hard work make a good relationship, not time. An equal partnership makes a great successful team. You need to be there and count on each other. You need to feel you are not taken advantage of. Relationships are about give and take, and sharing and caring. The following is a comparison of healthy vs. unhealthy relationships:

Healthy	vs.	**Unhealthy**
Trust	vs.	Mistrust
Honesty	vs.	Manipulation
Respect	vs.	Disrespect
Accountability	vs.	Blame
Communication	vs.	Control

Flexibility/negotiation	vs.	Rigidness/Power struggle
Understanding	vs.	Critical
Independent/Individual	vs.	Dependent/Ownership
Equality	vs.	Selfishness

Trust vs. Mistrust

Healthy relationships begin with trust. You are able to trust each other enough to be vulnerable. You can trust your partner to be faithful. You can trust each other completely with your thoughts, dreams, goals, ideas and feelings. Without trust, there is no foundation for a strong, healthy relationship.

Kristin and Rich were married for three years. They were having problem committing. They were beginning to turn away from each other. One day after an argument Kristin had lunch with a male friend, it turned into a one-night affair. Kristin felt terrible and knew she made a major mistake. She told Rich about it the next day. He was hurt and devastated. They began counseling to work through the pain of infidelity and rebuilding the trust back in their relationship. Trust is vital in relationships. Once it is broken, if it can be repaired, it takes a long time to repair the damages and rebuild trust again.

Honesty vs. Manipulation

Honesty is an important component to a relationship. Be honest with your feelings, needs and wants. Be open with each other so that you can share anything about yourself and your life. There is no fear in sharing. Without honesty, your relationship is based on manipulation. In manipulation you don't ask for what you need, instead, you connive or manipulate.

Peggy was married to Ted who was a manic-depressant. He refused to take his medication and continually drank and smoked pot. Peggy confronted him many times during their 10 year marriage about his drinking and drug use. She would beg him to go to counseling and a doctor for medication. Ted always promised, Peggy always wanted to believe his promises, but nothing ever changed. She'd threaten to leave, and many times she did. He'd make promises to stop drinking and drugging and make appointments to go to counseling and the doctor. He never followed through with his promises. Their marriage was a lie. She finally was able to see the manipulation and left him. He continued to drink and use drugs and he never sought help but kept he calling and making promises if she would return.

Respect vs. Disrespect

Respect helps the relationship grow. You must be able to respect your partner and what your partner stands for. You respect their thoughts, feelings, ideas and opinions. You show them respect in everything you say and do. You never disrespect your partner, not in words or in actions. This must be mutual. You don't always have to agree but you must be able to respect each other.

Steve and Debra came in for relationship counseling. He was totally disrespectful of Donna's thoughts, feelings, ideas, needs, and opinions. He was disrespectful even the way he spoke to her. She was so use to his disrespectful comments and behavior that she accepted them as the norm. When she felt she had enough, she'd fight back and she would scream and yell at him. Every time I confronted him in counseling he'd become upset. He said he was set in his ways. He really didn't want to change and didn't see any reason why he should. All he wanted to change was for her to stop screaming at him. They dropped out after three visits.

Accountability vs. Blame

This means each of you can hold yourself accountable for your actions without having your relationship in jeopardy. Neither of you sits in judgment and blames, but rather you confront and discuss problems openly. You can make mistakes and not expect your partner to put you down. You do hold each other accountable for your own actions. When you do disagree or fight, you fight fairly.

Terese and Phil blamed each other every time something went wrong. They both had legitimate and valid issues. The problem was they only saw how things affected themselves. In counseling, they would constantly interrupt each other. They sat their stewing and not really listening to their partner. They couldn't wait until they could tell their version. They worked very hard in counseling and made positive changes. They now listen without interrupting (most of the time) and hold themselves and each other accountable for their feelings and actions. They talk things out instead of getting angry or blaming each other for anything that goes wrong.

Communication vs. Control

Communication lines must always be open. You need to share openly with each other about anything and everything. You must be willing to share feelings, thoughts and desires. When there is a problem, you communicate, and talk it out. You never ignore it. You work on solutions to your problems together. Without open communication, everything becomes an issue of control. Keeping things in causes outburst later. This doesn't solve anything, and it creates more problems.

When Cherie and Gregg got angry at each other they wouldn't talk for days, at times, even weeks. They would ignore each other, even sleep in separate beds. They would not talk it out. Days or weeks later, they would gradually talk to each other. They were like two emotional volcanoes that could erupt at any time over anything. They both came into the marriage with unresolved baggages of anger. They were quick to take their anger out on each other. They worked individually on their unresolved issues and worked as a couple in counseling. They worked very hard at communicating and made major changes.

Flexibility and negotiation vs. Rigidness/Power Struggle

Flexibility and negotiation are major ingredients in a healthy relationship. You will not always agree. There must be give and take. Don't be so stuck in only one way. Your partner may do things differently. It doesn't necessarily make one right and the other wrong. It may be just different. Be flexible and negotiate to keep things fair. Don't get into power struggles. Don't keep score. You're a team working together. Never be abusive.

Donna and Jack were constantly in a power struggle. Donna had been in therapy dealing with unresolved abuse issues. Donna needed space and time to work through those issues. Jack felt like he was a casualty of war. Indeed they were both hurting. Both Donna and Jack were very rigid in their beliefs. For them, negotiating meant losing themselves and giving in to the other. Learning to be more flexible and negotiate during trying times allows you the time to work through the inside or the outside struggles that keep getting in the way of your relationship.

Understanding vs. Critical

Every relationship needs understanding. Don't be critical or judgmental. Be empathic and treat your partner the way you want to be treated. Even when you disagree you can still be respectful and understanding. Try to put yourself in your partner's place before you react or respond when there is a problem. You do not need to overreact. Be supportive when you can. When the chips are down make sure that you are available to your partner.

Dee and Rick were married five years. Dee was extremely critical. She was quick to judge Rick. She constantly put him down for doing things differently. Rick never confronted her about her criticalness. Dee never realized how critical she was of Rick. She was recreating the same thing her mother did to her father. Tearfully, she said, "I hated how she treated my father, how could I have not seen I was doing the same thing?" Without understanding the issues or problems in a relationship, we continue to engage in self-defeating behaviors or recreate the unhealthy behaviors from our history.

Independent/Individual vs. Dependent/Ownership

You must be able to be an individual but also be part of a relationship. You mustn't lose your identity. You need to have your independence but also know how to be a couple. You can have separate thoughts, interests, feelings and friends, but you learn how to meld them together. The two becomes a pair.

As the wedding unity candle symbolizes, there is one candle on each side of the large candle. They represent each of you as an individual. Then both of you light the middle one, representing the two of you as one. You don't lose your identity but you learn to become one. Healthy relationships leave room for independence and don't foster dependence. You are partners, not owners of possessions.

Mike is an 18 year old young man who was very domineering with his girlfriend. He wanted to pick her friends and tell her where to work. He admitted that he didn't want her to be friends with anyone that didn't like him. He admitted he use to be mentally and verbally abusive to her. Her friends told her to leave him. He has not been abusive since, but he knows her friends still don't like him. I helped Mike understand that his controlling and domineering behavior were cover-ups for his fears. He was afraid of losing her. His jealousy, insecurity and fear of abandonment was why he was so controlling. He began to realize if he didn't make changes he would lose her. Once you understand the underlying feelings you can begin to deal with the problem and change the behavior.

Equality vs. Selfishness

Relationships are about partnership. You treat your partner as you want to be treated. You do things for your partner as you know

117

your partner will do for you. Equality is not about possessions and bottom line totals. It's about togetherness, oneness. Equality has balance. It's two-way. If you entered into a partnership to begin a company wouldn't you expect that both of you equally participate? What would happen to the company and the partnership if one did all the work and made all the investment? A relationship is a partnership. You work together if you want it to be successful.

Shirley and Don came in for marriage counseling. Shirley was justifiably angry at Don for many things that occurred earlier in their marriage. Don had not understood how Shirley had felt. Shirley felt taken advantage of and not appreciated by Don. He realized he was not participating in childrearing or household duties. He began to understand his part in the problem of the relationship and why Shirley felt the way she did. He was taking, but not giving.

What do you expect from your relationship and are you getting it?

_____

_____

What do you want and need to see changed in your relationship?

_____

_____

A healthy relationship is about give and take. Sharing and caring. It's reciprocal. When you need your partner they seem to sense it and be there for you. If you are too deeply into what you need, what you want, what's important to you, then you will not be able to have an equal partnership. You must learn how to give of yourself and not be selfish. There is a time and place for selfishness but it should be the exception not the rule.

TEN COMMANDMENTS FOR A LOVING RELATIONSHIP

Above all, follow God's Golden Rule. Do unto others as they would do unto you.

1. Thou shall accept your partner the way they are.
✎ Don't try to change your partner into something they are not. Accept your partner as you would want your partner to accept you. This, of course, is different with abuse. No one deserves to be abused or should accept being abused.

2. Thou shall not guilt.
✎ When you don't get what you want or need, don't use guilt as a tactic to manipulate. If you don't like to be manipulated, don't manipulate your partner.

3. Thou shall honor and respect your partner.
✎ Respect your partner's opinions, thoughts, feelings and needs. Treat your partner the way you want to be treated. Remember to appreciate each other. Don't take each other for granted. Be respectful to your partner at all times. There must be mutual respect.

4. Thou shall compromise and be flexible.
✎ Don't keep score. A healthy relationship is a balance between give and take. Occasionally, do special things for each other, even when you don't want to. Don't be selfish. Take turns. Your partner's needs and wants are just as important as yours. Compromise and share without compromising yourself.

5. Thou shall not be demanding and controlling.
✎ Respect their right to say "no" and "I don't want to." Remember, your way is not the only way. Ask, don't demand. Give, don't just take. Respect each other's differences.

6. **Thou shall communicate feelings openly and honestly.**

   ✎ Don't go to bed angry or leave the house and stay away over night. Don't give your partner the silent treatment. Deal with problems openly and be honest with your feelings. Don't stuff your feelings and don't ignore your partner's feelings.

7. **Thou shall not dump baggage or "should" all over your partner.**

   ✎ Do not "should" on your partner. If you don't like to be "should" on, don't "should" on your partner. Don't dump or throw baggages of guilt at each other. Take and face responsibility for your own baggage and you own part of the problem.

8. **Thou shall be patient and kind.**

   ✎ Words can hurt very deeply and some words can never be forgotten. If you're upset or angry, take a time out to cool off. Think before you speak. You will not always think alike. Respect each other's differences and be considerate of each other's needs and feelings.

9. **Thou shall forgive trespasses.**

   ✎ If either of you does something wrong or makes a mistake, take responsibility for it. Make amends. Work it out. Forgive and move on. (If serious, seek professional help.) If something continues to bother you, deal with it immediately. Don't hold grudges. Talk it out. Don't stay angry.

10. **Thou shall love your partner with all your heart and soul.**

    ✎ Don't miss a moment to say "I love you" or to show your partner you love them. Let your words and actions be the same. Life is short. In a second, a life can be taken away. Love each other unconditionally. Be there for each other at all times. Don't take each other for granted.

If you follow the golden rule, you will have a healthy, loving relationship. Relationships, whether in a business or with a partner for life, must be respected and not neglected. Good relationships don't just happen. You must nurture them everyday. A relationship is like a flower garden. If you tend to it, nurture it, allow it to grow under ideal conditions, it will be beautiful and continue to blossom. If you neglect it, it dies.

A simple rule of thumb is treat others the way you want to be treated. You would not neglect or ignore your own company. You would not risk letting your company crumble because of a bad, impulsive decision. You would think things through before you made decisions. You would weigh consequences. Any relationship can crumble because of neglect or abandonment. To make a relationship successful, you must put your heart and soul in it, and work hard at making it grow. It needs commitment.

The person who doesn't take the relationship seriously and is unable to make a commitment to it will eventually lose it. No relationship is perfect. You will not always agree with each other's thoughts, ideas and opinions. Look for a balance, not perfection. Relationships are about two, not just one.

If your relationship is in trouble, don't be quick to quit. Seek help. If there is abuse, seek help with or without him/her.

Things I need to change to make my relationship healthy.

_____

_____

_____

I would like to end with this poem. The author is unknown.

We are, each of us, a miracle, unique in our own way.
Each day is made special by what we bring to it,
The joy, the caring, the closeness we share,
our rich pasts, and varied experiences.
We explore our differences
and become closer to each other
as we celebrate the gift of friendship
and the miracle of ourselves.

Chapter Ten

Finding a Balance

- *Chapter Ten* -

Finding a Balance

Life has many ups and downs. There is joy, happiness, sadness and pain in life. You can't have happiness without sadness, or joy without pain. It is all part of life. Finding a balance is the solution, but that is not easy. It's not how many times you fall that's important, it's that you keep getting up. It is easy to get trapped into "extreme" thinking. One extreme or the other can be unhealthy.

Personalities are made up of different components. Who you are is a mixture of different characteristics, genetics, assets and abilities. Your personality has many facets. There are the physical, emotional, intellectual, psychological, sexual and spiritual parts. There are the responsible adult and the child components. They must all equally blend and find a healthy balance.

You cannot define yourself by your characteristics or abilities alone. What happens to the athlete or the great body when they are no longer defined by that? Unless they have developed other components, they may become depressed or experience anxiety. Or they may try to live through their children or live in the past. They may be unable to move forward and be happy or content with themselves.

124

You are not just your emotions. You would feel overwhelmed every time you had a feeling. Your emotions would control you. Who you are is more than just your feelings. You have to be able to control your feelings and not have your feelings control you.

If you were just your intellect you would be a robot. Not to mention, egotistical, pompous, and boring. You would see only what is logical and rational and only look at facts. It is very difficult to have a relationship with someone like that. Your partner could be sick in a hospital but your partner's priority would be to attend the business meeting because it was the logical thing to do.

Although your psyche is also an important part of your personality, you can't analyze and interpret everything. Your psychological part allows you to look beyond things to better understand yourself and others. If you acted only from your psyche, you'd be overwhelmed with what's underneath everything, you'd ignore what's right in front of you. You would obsess with finding meaning, reasoning and understanding in everything, and you'd lose yourself in the process.

While your sexuality is an important part of who you are, you are not just your sexuality. People have committed suicide because they could not live with sexual desires that were different from others. Some have such an obsession with their sexuality that they are not monogamous. They hurt people they love because of it. Some have a sickness and have abused others to meet their needs. Some have such a perversion of sexuality that other people become victims of their perversions.

You are not just your spirituality. Many people appear to be spiritual, yet for some it is just a facade. Your spiritual side helps you weather many a storm. It lends guidance, support and faith when you are lost. Heaven knows, it's a very important part of your personality. True spirituality comes from within.

125

Inside your personality is also the adult and child component. The adult part thinks logically, rationally, reasonably and is responsible. For some, the adult may also be critical and judgmental. The child part doesn't think. It's emotional, intuitive and not always able to put things in perspective. You need a balance. You cannot live your adult life thinking and acting as a child.

Finding a balance is about being able to see both sides and finding the middle. You need to blend all ingredients in your personality. If you do not find a balance in what you do, you become trapped. Some people are overly responsible. They take responsibility for everyone and everything and all times. Others take no responsibility at all. Each extreme is unhealthy. You have to find your own balance. Some take what everyone says so personally, that they try to please everyone and ignore what they want. Yet others, couldn't care less what others think, and does everything they want without caring about anyone else's needs or wants. Again, you need balance. Taking care of yourself doesn't mean ignoring everyone else.

Even good statements that you were brought up with can be taken to the extreme. Remember Thumper's words, "If you have nothing nice to say, don't say anything." Of course, you don't want uncaring people saying hurtful things. Yet, some people take advantage of you and your good nature because you would never say anything to them. You have to find the right balance for each situation. Remember the old expression, you don't want to throw the baby out with the bathwater. Find a balance.

One person's perception may not be the same as yours. Just because someone says it, doesn't mean it's true. If someone says you're selfish, it may mean you are not doing it their way. Be objective. You need to look at both sides. Maybe you are being selfish, and maybe you're not. Be honest with yourself. Listen and hear what people say, then look within for your answer. Don't let others define who you are, but don't ignore messages either. Find a balance, find the right blend that works for you.

Sometimes you have to get lost in order to find yourself. Of course this does not mean, leave your family behind and go searching for the answers in life. Find a way to be responsible and still take care of themselves. Remember, there are consequences to your choices.

What about the 70's era, when emphasis was on doing everything for yourself and being true to yourself? It created the infamous "Me Generation." There must be a balance. You need to take responsibility for the way you think, feel and act. You need to recognize that all choices have consequences, good and bad. You need to take people and consequences into consideration before you make decisions or choices. It is just as unhealthy to think of yourself only as it is to think only of others and ignore yourself.

Life is not always easy. Things don't always go as planned. Sometimes it's hard to cope and get through a day. But with adulthood there comes responsibility. Especially if you have children. History does repeat itself. The choices you make impact and influence each new generation. Find a way to balance your family and your life.

Many times I see children of the parents who couldn't cope but wanted children anyway. Or the parent who didn't think their lifestyle or drug or alcohol use should change because they had children. Those children are affected by such choices. This affects the next generation. You must take responsibility for your actions and the life you choose to lead. Whatever path you are on, you have chosen the roads that led you there.

Children, however, are on the path where you put them. Your choices affect them. Think of the effects and consequences of your thoughts, feelings and actions. In order to find balance in yourself and the world, recognize that you can't change others or the world. Make changes within yourself.

The following are words that were inscribed in the Crypts of Westminster Abbey in 1100 AD. The author was unknown.

When I was young and free and my imagination had no limits,
I dreamed of changing the world. As I grew older and wiser,
I discovered the world would not change, so I shortened my sights
Somewhat and decided to change only my country.
But it too, seemed immovable.

As I grew into my twilight years, in one last desperate attempt, I
settled for changing only my family, those closest to me, but alas,
They would have none of it. And now as I lie on my deathbed,
I suddenly realized:

If I had only changed myself first, then by example I would have
Changed my family. From their inspiration and encouragement,
I would then have been able to better my country and who knows,
I may have even changed the world.

Everyone has ups and downs. No one escapes tragedy and trauma. The key to having peace of mind and being happy is not letting everything get to you. As the Serenity Prayer says "Accept the things you cannot change and change the things you can." Many times you worry about things that may never occur. Ask yourself, "In six months, how important will this be?"

Finding a balance isn't always easy. Your emotions, intellect, spirituality and sexuality can feel overwhelming. There really is no simple solution or easy way to follow. What works on Monday doesn't necessarily work on Tuesday. What works with one person doesn't necessarily work for another. You will not always handle things the same way. For some things, you can say, "Oh well." Other things are more serious and you have to take responsibility to handle it. As the Serenity Prayer says, "Lord help me to have the wisdom to know the difference."

As for me, I have God in my life. My daily prayers help keep me grounded. I also need the love of my family and friends. I believe that people who are not happy get trapped in their problems and don't know how to get out. For me, God is the way out. If you don't know Him, just reach out to Him.

Prayer of Thomas Merton

My Lord God, I have no idea where I am going. I do not see the road ahead of me. I cannot know for certain where it will end. Nor do I really know myself, and the fact that I think that I am folloiwng your will does not mean that I am actually doing so. But I believe that the desire to please you does in fact please you. And I hope I have that desire in all that I am doing. I hope that I will never do anything apart from that desire. And I know that as I do this you will lead me by the right road though I may know nothing about it. Therefore will I trust you always though I may seem to be lost and in the shadow of death. I will not fear, for you are ever with me, and you will never leave me to face my perils alone.

I hope that this book has given you the insight to better understand yourself. I hope the tips were helpful. Whether you laughed, cried or were simply amused by the examples and stories, I hope they have inspired, motivated or helped you learn from them. We hold on to and carry too much baggage. This definitely prevents us from going where we want to go, doing what we want to do and being who we want to be.

It's time you move forward. Regardless of your past experiences, take responsibility for your thoughts, feelings, actions and your life. When the road gets bumpy, ask God or your higher power for help. Don't ignore His direction. Don't be afraid to do the right thing for others. Find a balance in doing for others and for yourself. I wish each of you good health and happiness. Go forward, not backwards.

I would like to end with a poem. The author is unknown.

One of the hardest lessons to learn is how to let go - let go of people, of the past, of so many things, good and bad, that daily touch our lives.

Ready or not, we must learn to let go. But, the beauty of this is that, by letting go of some things, we open our lives and make ourselves ready for the exciting arrival of something new—
and letting go becomes something special—
A beginning.

Affirmations

Affirmations are powerful, positive mental message. They are messages about feelings, behavior, and beliefs. Words can be dynamic tools that encourage and heal. These affirmations will enhance any adult's life. The affirmations provide people with a new way of seeing themselves, other people, their relationships, and a larger view of life and the environment in which they live.

Affirmations should be repeated several times a day for at least twenty days. You can carry a small piece of paper with the affirmation written on it, post it in front of you at work, put it in your car, place it on your mirror, and eventually the things you are affirming will become a reality.

These affirmations were submitted by my student, Lora Lee Landrume Loss, and I thank her for her permission to use them:

1 *Letting go of baggage:*
   "By letting go of WHAT I was yesterday, I can be and appreciate WHO I am today."

2. *Understanding self-defeating behaviors:*
   'Today, I choose not to linger in negativity, but rather to practice a positive attitude and outlook."

3. *Understanding and dealing with overwhelming feelings:*
   "I can accept this not as a sure defeat, but as a challenge and overcome it."

4. *Learning to let go of guilt and shame:*
"I can own my guilt by turning it into responsibility. Shame, on the other hand, is not mine to own, so I give it up."

5. *Learning to set limits and boundaries*:
"Knowing who I am allows me to set limits, not to be trapped in them. I am as capable or as incapable as I believe myself to be."

6. *Building and re-creating self-esteem:*
"I am, therefore I am worthy. I can if I believe in me."

7. *Communicating in assetive ways:*
"No, can mean I love me enough to love you. Yes, can mean the same."

8. *Taking control of your attitude and how you are thinking:*
"MY thinking can cripple or empower me. Today I can stay stuck in the unacceptable or rise to and embrace the acceptable."

9. *Relationships: Unhealthy vs. healthy:*
"How can I say I love you without saying, 'I'?"

10. *Finding a balance:*
"I am building the framework of a healthier me by practicing balance in every aspect of my daily living."

Bibiography

Barksdale, L.S. *Building Self-Esteem*. Idyllwild, CA: The Barksdale Foundation. 714-659-4676.

Beattie, Melody. *Beyond Codependency*.

Canfield, Jack and Mark Victor Hansen. *Chicken Soup for the Soul Series*. Deerfield Beach FL: Health Communication, Inc.

Fossom and Mason. *Facing Shame*.

Jeffers, Susan. *Feel the Fear and Do It Anyway*, NY: Fawcett Columbine.

Greenberger & Padesky. *Mind Over Mood*. New York, NY: Guilford Press Publishing.

Larson, Ernie. *Life Beyond Addiction: Understanding the Basics of Recovery*.

Melody, Pia. *Facing Codependence*.

Middleton-Mozz, Jane. *Shame and Guilt: Masters of Disguise*.